SPEAKING ABOUT THE PAST
Oral History for 5-7 year olds

Sandip Hazareesingh
*with **Penny Kenway** and **Kelvin Simms***

A Resource for Teachers
Building Blocks Early Years Education Project

tb

Trentham Books in association with **Save the Children**

First published in 1994 by Trentham Books Limited

Trentham Books Limited
Westview House
734 London Road
Oakhill
Stoke-on-Trent
Staffordshire
England ST4 5NP

British Cataloguing in Publication Data
A catalogue record for this book is available from the British Library.

ISBN: 1 85856 023 3

Cover: St. Pancras Hotel and Station from Pentonville Road: Sunset, by John O'Connor, 1884. Courtesy: Museum of London.

Back cover: A mounted prince begging water from four women at a well, somewhere in north India, about 1720.
Courtesy of the Trustees of the V&A.

Designed and typeset by Trentham Print Design Limited, Chester and printed in Great Britain by Bemrose Shafron Limited, Chester

We would like to thank the following people and organisations for their help and support:

The children and staff of Maybury County First School, Woking, Surrey. The children and staff of St. Michael's School, Camden, London. The children and staff of Wellington Primary School, Hounslow, Middlesex. Rebecca Handy, Emma Webb, Sylvia Collicott, Sallie Purkis, Margot Brown, Margaret Lally, Pat Hughes, Rose Drury, Shahida Usman, Miriam Steiner, Iram Siraj-Blatchford, Viv Edwards, Sheila Wolfendale, Jane Oxley, Usha Bahl, Dorothy Rouse, Jenny Williams, Linda McGill, Dorit Braun, Hilary Hester, Sheila Taylor, Yvette Fields, Janine Wooster, Gavin Morgan, Sue McAlpine, Isobel Sinden.

The Museum of London. Commonwealth Institute. London Transport Museum. Victoria & Albert Museum. Gunnersbury Museum. Reading & Language Information Centre, University of Reading. Centre for Language in Primary Education, London. London Division, Save the Children Fund.

Special thanks to Dorothy Illing for all her work on the manuscript.

SPEAKING ABOUT THE PAST

Oral history for 5–7 year olds

A resource for teachers

Contents

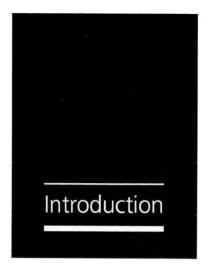

Introduction

Speaking About the Past is designed for all primary teachers and children (Key Stage 1 in England and Wales) and is especially sensitive to the needs of bilingual children who, in the course of their everyday lives, use more than one language with some degree of confidence.

The book aims to help teachers create a historically-based framework for learning within which children can develop through talking, listening, thinking, picture and print reading, visual observation, remembering, imagining, feeling, handling, writing, drawing, painting, designing, constructing, modelling and role-play...

Particular emphasis is placed on narrative, talk and discussion. Children find it easy to communicate ideas and emotions through oral language and are motivated to engage actively in interpreting the historical evidence in front of them. Oracy also enables a multiplicity of people to tell their stories in their own words and voices. It brings history to life in all its rich variety of perspectives.

Although we focus on history, all the activities described here are also cross-curricular. It is indeed characteristic of children's learning in the early years that, while we may put in a lot of history, children quite often respond with a good deal of language or art.

The activities can be used flexibly and are designed to fit in with the learning situations which already occur in the classroom.

Speaking About the Past and the National Curriculum

History is essentially about the study of people, of people in the past. As the National Curriculum Council's Non-statutory Guidance for History points out:

The past influences all aspects of our lives. It shapes the customs and beliefs of the communities to which we belong. Learning about the past and the methods used to study it helps pupils make sense of the world in which they live.

There is also the stated objective that:

National Curriculum history requires pupils to be taught about the cultural and ethnic diversity of past societies and the experiences of men and women. Through history pupils acquire understanding and respect for other cultures and values. They should develop what the History Working Group called 'the quality of open-mindedness which questions assumptions and demands evidence for points of view.

Key Stage 1 National Curriculum history consists of a single study unit made up of the following elements or 'sources': stories, eyewitness accounts of past happenings, artefacts, pictures and photographs, adults talking about their own past, written sources, buildings.

The Dearing Review of the National Curriculum has reduced the history attainment targets from three ('knowledge and understanding of history', 'interpretations of history', and 'the use of historical sources') to just one, defined simply as 'history'. The stated objective is to break down the artificial divide between knowledge, understanding and skills and to reduce the burden of recording and assessment at the end of the key stage. The History Curriculum's developmental orientation is maintained in the new Level Descriptions (see chapter seven) which sets out progressively higher levels of achievement through the key stage.

While welcoming the National Curriculum's emphasis on the need for continuity and progression in developing and evaluating children's historical understanding, as well as its supportive comments on cultural diversity, *Speaking About the Past* offers a perspective which is much more explicitly based on an awareness of the importance of starting with the child.

There is a particular focus on children's own origins in a particular family, language and culture. This is supported by the NCC circular number 6 on cross-curricular dimensions which emphasises the importance of personal and social development through the curriculum.

History speaks in many voices, fashioning different versions of the past for each one of us. The actual range of children from a variety of cultural and linguistic backgrounds in contemporary British society make these stories more diverse than ever.

This book suggests that the Key Stage 1 programme of study can be centred around stories, family narratives, pictures and photographs, artefacts and visits. The activities are, moreover, designed to suggest the rich possibilities of a genuinely multicultural and multilingual approach to history in the early years and are consistent with the advice offered in NCC Curriculum Guidance 8 on Education for Citizenship.

Curriculum provision should build on personal experience and encourage pupils to see citizenship as something which extends beyond their immediate experiences and relationships. Individuals have obligations to and relationships with national, European and world-wide communities.

(National Curriculum Council, *Curriculum Guidance 8: Education for Citizenship* 1990 p. 15)

Key Ideas underlying the activites

❑ In the early years children learn about the past through a regressive rather than chronological approach. This means they start from the present and the very recent past and move gradually to the more distant past and to times beyond living memory.

❑ Children's understanding of themselves, their origins, cultural experiences and family history is a good starting point for the development of their historical thinking.

❑ Children should have the opportunity to explore a variety of types of evidence, in particular stories, images, artefacts, people as well as places of historic interest.

❑ These sources enable children to engage with and enjoy the past, to see it as alive, exciting and worth discovering.

❑ Oral language is a crucial dimension of historical understanding. Spontaneous discussion helps children to interpret the various types of evidence and promotes concept development.

❑ Provision should be made for development, alongside English, of the child's first language, usually the language of his or her past experience.

❑ Children develop historical concepts and skills through trial and error, speculation and the gradual building up of experience and memory, rather than through the imposition of ready-made facts and interpretations.

❑ Parents' and grandparents' knowledge of their own and their children's past is a rich resource that schools can draw on.

❑ Developing the historical aspect of the curriculum provides excellent opportunities for strengthening home-school links.

❑ The development of historical attitudes, concepts and skills supports learning in all areas of the curriculum

Attitudes	Concepts	Skills
Self-esteem	Sequence	Memory and recall
Curiosity	Duration	Oral descriptive/narrative
Enjoyment	Continuity/change	Language of time
Eagerness to communicate	Difference/similarity	Visual literacy
Concern for people	Agedness	Picture reading
Valuing different cultures	Cause/effect	Imaginative
Care for the environment	Time	Reasoning/questioning
Motivation to find out more	Frequency	Sequencing
Awareness of different perspectives	Co-operation/conflict	Drawing/painting
	Evidence	Reading
		Writing/word processing

Overview of contents

Parents and the child's past

...offers a number of strategies and hints about how schools and teachers can work with parents in developing the historical dimension of the curriculum. There is particular emphasis on participatory activities and events which can potentially draw parent's experience and knowledge into the school curriculum.

The past through topic work

...covers the planning of the topic to ensure that the historical aspect is given equal weight and that children's cultural experiences are fully taken into account. Three examples of topic-based activities are provided.

Recall and empathy: fictional stories

...focuses on stories as a key source in developing children's historical attitudes, concepts and skills. Eight easily available stories have been highlighted and cross-curricular activity webs developed from each one. Between them, the stories are multicultural, gender sensitive and available in a range of languages. Each one offers rich possibilities for children to empathise with characters, imagine different worlds and also to recall and talk about their own past experiences. Other useful stories are discussed in section eight.

Remembering the past: personal memories and family narratives

...suggests ways of encouraging children to research their family history and to reflect on changes and continuities, differences and similarities between their own lives and the childhoods of older members of their family.

Picturing the past: images

...highlights images as a primary source of evidence that help children to see aspects of the past in concrete terms. This again allows comparisons between the present and earlier periods. Ten pictures are provided: six photographs: four of London scenes in the 1910s, 20s, 30s and 40s; and two of Suffragette demonstrations, in 1908 and 1911; four paintings: two of London streets in the nineteenth century, one sixteenth century early Mughal, and one eighteenth century late Mughal, both depicting scenes in north India.

Experiencing the past: artefacts and visits

...focuses on the importance of children experiencing the past through observing, visiting, handling and exploring traces of former times. There is particular emphasis on ways of discovering that are enjoyable and motivating.

Assessing children's achievements

...considers defining a basis for assessing children's development of historical concepts and skills, as well as what might be regarded as evidence of the child's achievements.

More stories and useful books

...provides a broad selection of readily obtainable good stories to complement the story-based activities in section three, together with a selection of information books for children about the past.

Finding out more...

The activities described here are starting points, providing a basic set of ideas to be adapted to the particular situation in which you work. This final section aims to provide information which will enable teachers to develop historical activities and ideas further in the light of their own expertise and enthusiasms.

Chapter one

Parents and the child's past

Parents have most knowledge and understanding of their child. A crucial dimension of this knowledge is their familiarity with their child's past experience. Aspects of this meaningful past include:

- ❑ the origins and meaning of the child's name
- ❑ the languages used and heard by the child in different family situations
- ❑ important family celebrations
- ❑ special occasions which the child has a fond recollection of
- ❑ home routines
- ❑ favourite things, eg toys, games, objects, foods, television programmes
- ❑ favourite days and times of the day
- ❑ regular trips
- ❑ journeys and visits to places
- ❑ well-loved fictional stories and/or family narratives

Enabling children to talk about and recall these experiences helps to foster self-esteem and begins to develop their understanding of a range of historical concepts: sequence, time, change/continuity. It is therefore important to provide opportunities for parents to share with the teacher their knowledge of their child's experiences and of the past more generally.

Parents' perception of the school and the curriculum and their willingness and confidence in contributing to their child's school learning is likely to be influenced by a number of factors including:

- ❏ their own experience, or non-experience, of formal education
- ❏ their understanding of the early years curriculum
- ❏ their feelings about the school environment
- ❏ their expectations of school and teachers
- ❏ the nature and accessibility of the information provided by the school
- ❏ their degree of fluency in both their first language and English
- ❏ work and family commitments
- ❏ the discriminations and difficulties they may be facing in their everyday lives.

At a time of enormous change in the education system, it is more than ever essential for schools and teachers to make explicit their policies and curricula. A whole-school commitment to sharing knowledge and information with parents, providing regular opportunities for discussion and feedback, will enhance parents' understanding of what they are requested to contribute. Indeed, some schools already provide opportunities for parents to gain hands-on experiences of the curriculum.

There are a variety of formal and informal ways of developing curriculum-based links with parents:

Through existing forms of developmental record-keeping

Records currently used in many parts of the country emphasise the importance of developing an assessment partnership between home and school as a means of ensuring continuity and progression in the child's learning experiences.

The *Primary Learning Record*, for instance, provides a framework for recording as much information as possible about children's development in their first languages as well as in English. It enables teachers to fulfil the requirements of the National

---

PRIMARY LEARNING RECORD

Teachers should bear in mind LEA policies on Equal Opportunities (eg race, gender and class) and on special educational needs in completing each section of the record

School   Year group

Name   DOB

Languages understood   Languages written
Languages spoken   Languages read

Details of any aspects of hearing, vision, coordination   Names of staff involved with child's learning development
or other special needs affecting the child's learning.
Give the source and the date of this information.

PART A to be completed during the Autumn term

A1 Record of discussion between child's parent(s) and class teacher

Curriculum, while progressively compiling a much fuller picture of a bilingual child as a learner than can be gained by monitoring performance in English alone.

Completed in sequence over the autumn, spring and summer terms in collaboration with parents and children, it potentially enables teachers to find out about the home-related areas of the child's experience, as listed on page five. (See also chapter nine *Finding out more.*)

Through providing opportunities for parents to understand and contribute to the school curriculum

a. Sharing books

Most schools enable children to choose story or information books to take home and share with their parents and families. Whether or not in the context of a formal reading scheme, the accompanying record card should provide space for both teachers and parents (or another adult or older brother or sister) to comment on the child's use of the book or other aspects of the learning experience.

Simple headings, accompanied by clear visual symbols (especially useful for parents who do not read fluently) make for an easy and informal dialogue. Teachers can tap the wealth of knowledge parents have of their own children, while the home sharing of a story between child and parent can stimulate conversations about the child's school experience.

Parents who do not read confidently in any language may need reassurance. Point out that there are many ways in which they can support their child's enjoyment of books and interest in reading: by listening, making sense of the story through the pictures, asking questions in their first language, prompting responses and discussing sequences or events.

Choosing good stories (see chapter three) is vital in sustaining this exchange. Include a range of historical stories, as listed in chapter eight.

b. Workshops for parents

Many schools already hold workshops for parents on particular aspects of the curriculum. These sessions are usually flexibly organised, to accommodate parents' other commitments. Workshops can perform several functions:

❑ they help teachers to gain an insight into the range of skills parents may possess

❑ they help parents to develop their skills and confidence

❑ they to developing a mutually supportive relationship between home and school

❑ they enable parents to become familiar with what goes on in the classroom

❑ they help teachers to gain an insight into the child's meaningful home experiences

❑ they offer parents the motivating benefits of a finished product.

One nursery teacher decided to devise a set of cross-curricular matching, sorting and sequencing games for her class, using the children themselves as models. She took individual and group photographs of the class, engaged in sequences of everyday classroom activities. The teacher then invited parents to a workshop session and involved them in the practical making and eventual playing of the games with the children.

The parents helped to back the photos on card and cover them with clear film. They sorted the cards into manageable quantities for the children to play simple matching games, or laid them on the table face downwards to become a game of 'pairs'. They made baseboards for lotto games. Each baseboard consisted of photocopies of four of the photos, allowing for lotto games of increasing complexity to be played.

Photo-cards showing children engaged in daily activities were made into simple sequencing games, ranging from three to ten cards. Some photos were also enlarged and made into jigsaw puzzles, which could be cut into more pieces as the children mastered them.

The teacher explained that the educational purpose of the games was to encourage the development of the children's oral language skills, in both their first language and English. In the sequencing and classifying games, children could describe what was going on and explain their reasons for choosing a particular order or sorting in a particular way. The games were also important in terms of the development of their early reading and number skills.

Moreover, sequencing activities helped children to sort out the correct order of events in their everyday life. This involved the use of the language and conventions of time and helped children to begin to talk about their experiences in a historical way.

The parents were very enthusiastic about playing the games with their children and greatly enjoyed looking at the photos and laughing over them. Many felt that they could devise similar activities for their children at home. Because the games were based on images of themselves, the children were keen to play them. They were allowed to take the games home to play with their families.

c. Open events

Open events such as parents' evenings can combine a variety of purposes in the life of a school. Held regularly, they can fulfil a number of objectives:

- ❑ teachers can display children's work and achievements
- ❑ parents can discuss their child's progress with the teacher
- ❑ parents can see what actually happens in the classroom and understand just what is included in the school curriculum and why
- ❑ the school is able to launch new initiatives in a way that invites parental support and participation

Maybury County First School in Woking, Surrey, held an Open Afternoon for parents at the start of the summer term. The school enjoyed a good social relationship with parents: school trips and visits were very well supported and attendance was generally very high at assemblies, raffles, bazaars and sports days. The National Curriculum Orders for History and Geography had recently been published and the headteacher and staff wanted to draw on the parents' knowledge and understanding of their own and their children's pasts in developing the history curriculum.

All the classes were involved in preparing the work to be displayed in the hall, for the parents, children and teachers of the whole school to see. The Open Afternoon was held in the third week of term, to allow time for preparation.

At the end of the spring term a letter of invitation, in Urdu and English, was given out to parents and a reminder was sent out in the first week of the new term. Probably more successful, however, were the informal chats which teachers and the bilingual assistant took care to have with the parents before the event. The turn-out was very good, with parents chatting amongst themselves and to the teachers about the various displays.

The whole-school topic for the term was *Journeys*. One display showed a map of Britain and a map of the world, side by side, indicating the journeys made by each adult member of the school to come to live in Woking. Beside the maps, flags drawn and coloured by the children indicated the many countries of origin of the children and their families.

There was a blown-up version of the topic flow-chart, surrounded by pictures of different places and old forms of transport. Right at the bottom of this display, two Reception class children had drawn time-lines: drawings of *Important Journeys in Imran's Life* and *Important Journeys in Joanna's Life.*

There was also a display of story-books concerned with journeys and travel, including examples of stories to which parents had contributed in different ways. The bilingual captions read:

This is a story which parents have translated. Can you help us to translate some other stories?.. This is a story written by a mum for her child. Would you like to write a story for your child?.... This is a picture story about a child's first journey. Would you like to put words to the pictures?

Examples of artefacts were attractively set out on an old tablecloth, with a tape recorder beside them captioned:

1938! This is a taped story of when Mrs Irwin (the headteacher) *was a child. Would you like to do a taped story for us?*

A display focused on *Ways of communicating with family and friends who live in other places.* It featured drawings, postcards and letters written by the children, and cards sent on such special occasions as Eid, Diwali, Christmas, Chinese New Year, Hannukah, Easter.

One effect of the display was to move some parents to reminisce amongst themselves about old times. And the children spent a great deal of time browsing through the displays, particularly the pictures and story books. They often read to one another and discussed the images of the past at length, obviously stimulated by the resources on display.

Over the next eight weeks the parents, especially those from Reception/Y1 classes, contributed in different ways to the term's historical activities. They provided old photos and artefacts which contributed to the suitcase activity (see section seven). Others collaborated with their children to make tapes about a significant occasion in the child's recent past.

One grandad came to the class to tell the children about his wartime experiences as a soldier in the British Indian army. He spoke in Urdu and illustrated his talk with old photos of India taken in the 1940s. The bilingual assistant provided simultaneous English translation. Another parent recorded the session on tape.

One mum came in to work collaboratively with her child on writing a story. She helped her daughter to recall their holiday in Pakistan the previous summer, and they based the story on their memories. The daughter illustrated the story with her own drawings of what she had seen in Pakistan. Finally some parents began to work on translating monolingual stories.

Chapter two

The past through topic work

Classroom topics or themes generally refer to realities within the child's experience. The flexible, cross-curricular nature of topic work potentially enables children to relate their own experiences and interests to a far wider range of human experiences, both present and past. This allows children to move beyond themselves, an essential condition for successful learning. The historical dimension of the curriculum can quite easily be fitted into the most common topics used by teachers at Key Stage 1.

Some recommended topics:

Journeys, Homes, Toys, Families, Clothes/Costumes, Food, Celebrations, Ourselves, Our school, Our community, Communication, Machines, Growth, Light.

A whole staff working as a team to plan the topic and particularly its historical aspect will find it useful to consider the following:

Knowledge of the child

❏ How do you find out what the children already know and what they bring to the topic?

Breadth and Balance

❏ Is the topic sufficiently broad and balanced to

— enable the integral inclusion of a historical dimension within the full range of curriculum areas (might a topic on *journeys* have greater potential than one on *birds*)?

— offer children global and multicultural perspectives, consistent with the National Curriculum Council's advice on cross-curricular themes and dimensions?

Flexibility

❑ Is the topic delivered in such a way as to

— stimulate and motivate all children, enabling all the children to contribute their own particular ideas and insights?

— enable children to develop their own interests, offering them opportunities to discover what they would like to learn more about?

Subject strands and cross-curricular?

❑ How does the topic plan reconcile National Curriculum subject strands and attainment targets with the essentially cross-curricular nature of children's learning in the early years?

Historical sources

❑ Are there enough of the required Key Stage 1 historical sources available for children to use? If not, how might these resources be assembled?

Progression and differentiation

❑ Do activities provide both progression and differentiation, ie scope for children to progress towards the various level descriptions at the appropriate pace for each child?

Bilingual skills

❑ Do activities provide opportunities for bilingual children to use and develop their first languages as well as English?

Visits and multi-sensory learning

❑ Does the topic provide opportunities for visits and first-hand experiences of learning?

Parental involvement

❑ What potential does the topic offer for working in partnership with parents and for developing links with the local community?

The topic webs on the following pages illustrate how the historical elements can be integrated within cross-curricular schemes of work.

Stories as a key activity

A Balloon for Grandad; *Do You Believe in Magic?*
The Bird who was an Elephant; *When Grandma
came.* etc
Relating to children's own experiences/past
Practicing the language/ conventions of time/
place Why/When/What/Where journeys are
made
Feelings/emotions involved in journeys Letters to
friends/relations in other places Look and Read
programmes
(*Cross-curricular, esp. Language/History/
Geography*)

Types of Transport

Feet, Wings, Bicycles/Buses Cars/Rickshaws,
Trains/Lorries Ships/Boats, Aeroplanes/Balloons
Space Rockets What do they carry'? eg foods
from around the world
Designing boats to float
Devices to receive long distance sounds/images
(*Design/Tech/IT/Science/Maths*)

Drama/Movement/Music

Chipko dance and drama (Academy of Indian
Dance workshop)
'Hugging the trees' role-play
Dramatising travel stories
Musical instruments/sounds from around the
world
Sound effects to illustrate a journey/story Using
instruments to create sound journeys
(*Music/Physical Education/Art Science/Technology*)

Journeys into the past

Children interviewing parents
Parents in school, talking about their own past
Time-lines
Letters to grandparents/ grandparents' stories
Suitcase at left luggage
Imaginary expeditions
Artefacts from local museums, parents and
teachers Images of the past
(*History/Language/Maths*)

JOURNEYS

Local/National/Global journeys

Where we come from? (data/ graph work)
Exploring the school environment, local places,
landmarks (streets, shops, mosque, church,
gardens, fire station, canal)
Train journeys to nearby places (eg Guildford,
Southampton)
Other places: Birmingham, Bradford
Other countries: Pakistan, India
Exploring weather/seasons
Journey of pigeons (Geordie Racer)
Making maps Measuring distance
Plotting journeys on real maps
Interpreting symbols
(*Geography/History/Language Maths/Science/IT*)

Celebrations/Special Occasions

Journeys and celebrations
When/How people celebrate Ramadan/Easter/
Passover/Holi
Birthdays
Giving and receiving
Weddings
Life cycle: family rites, birth, growth, death
(*Religious Education/History/ Science/Maths*)

Creative

Children telling stories
Listening and drawing
Reading/writing
Making 3-D models
Colour mixing
Painting sketches
Visual appreciation skills
Making My journey books/illustrations
(*Whole Curriculum*)

Topic web: *Journeys*.
Maybury County First School, Woking

Stories as a key activity:

A Dark Dark Tale; Home Place; The Paperbag Prince; Our House. etc

Relating to children's own experiences of home, present and past. What is a home? Why do we need homes? Identifying the words for home in different languages.

Practicing the language of time and place

The planet Earth as our common home

(Language/History/Art/ Geography)

Creativity/Visual Literacy:

Children taking pictures of homes in the neighbourhood: collecting pictures from magazines, travel brochures etc. Writing stories

Children making a plan of their home, drawing and labelling the room they like best.

Painting/Drawing/Modelling/ collage of homes

Designing a house, items of furniture for particular rooms

Making prints, patterns and decorations for furnishings (eg using Indian block-prints)

Follow-up work from museum visit. Setting up a 'changing kitchen' in the classroom

(Art/Cross-Curricular)

Homes, local and global:

Photographs/discussion of children's own homes

Home to School (mapwork, charts. number, measure)

Exploring homes in the local environment (outings)

Homes in other places, countries (Bangladesh).

Children's own experiences, photographs/ images

Where are their homes? Similarities and differences

Exploring home artefacts from around the world (Commonwealth Institute Treasure Chest)

(Language/Geography/Maths/ History/Art/ IT)

HOMES

Special Focus: Kitchens

Bilingual story: *Mum's Strike.* How different is a kitchen to other rooms? Different images of kitchens. How cooking techniques and materials have changed.

Exploring a range of utensils and discussing their use

Cooking a culturally diverse range of dishes

(Language/Science/History/ Technology)

Homes In the Past:

Using images to identify changes in homes and home life 'then and now'. Old homes in the neighbourhood.

Spot the difference.

Handling household artefacts at the Museum of London, visiting the Victorian Galleries

Children interviewing parents.

Children writing to grandparents

Home time-lines

Investigating a suitcase of old household objects made up from contributions from parents, teachers and other adults in the school

Homes and Celebrations (Birthdays, Eid)

(History/Language/Art/RE/IT)

Types of home:

Flat, house, hut, caravan, tent, bungalow, boat.

How are homes made?

Different homes for different climates.

Exploring different sizes, materials used, styles of architecture, interior designs, furniture, methods of heating/lighting

(Science/Design/Tech/ Maths/Geography)

Drama/Music:

Listening to various kinds of music/dance and identifying their homes (origins)

Matching musical instruments with homes in different parts of the world

Making music with a variety of instruments

Role-play: characters from stories expressing emotions associated with home

(Music/Drama/Geography)

Topic web: *Homes.*

St. Michael's School, Camden

Stories as a key activity:

The Toymaker, The Hidden House, The Polka Dot Horse. etc

Relating to children's own experiences/past

Practising the language/conventions of time/place

Each child bringing in a favourite toy to talk about.

(Cross-Curricular, esp. History/ Geography/Language)

Play in the past:

Toy suitcase, made up of old toys from children's families and other adults in school

Images of old toys and games

Parents/grandparents talking about how they played as children

Visits to, eg Eureka Museum for Children, Bethnal Green Museum of Childhood

Exploring treasure chest of toys from the Commonwealth Institute

Toy timelines

(History/Language/Geography)

Drama:

Role-play based on stories

Playtime songs and rhymes from a variety of cultures

Making music from different instruments

(Language/P.E./Music)

Different kinds of playthings:

Ordinary objects, cuddly toys, construction toys, electronic toys, musical toys, wind-up toys, adult toys.. How are they made? Where do they come from? Which age groups play with them? Sorting/ matching/counting into sets according to type of play, materials, texture, shape, size. Exploring forces, investigating speed

(Design/Tech/Science/Maths/ Geography)

TOYS

Places of play:

Home, indoors, outdoors, classroom, playground, park, beach, on holiday. Identifying the different kinds and times of play What playthings can we find in/make from the local environment? Collecting natural play materials (Geography/Science/ Language)

Special Occasions/Sharing:

When do we give/receive toys? Who do we give toys to? Who do we share our playthings with? Playing a range of co-operative games Finding out about games from different parts of the world

(R.E./Education for Citizenship)

Creative:

Reading and retelling

Writing stories inspired by playing/toys

Visual literacy skills Drawings, paintings.

Designing and making toys from a variety of materials

Constructing and arranging a toy museum/shop

(Cross-curricular)

Topic web: *Toys*.
Caldecot Primary School, Lambeth

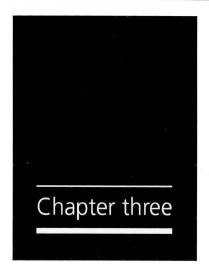

Chapter three

Recall and empathy: stories

Stories offer children insights into their own lives and help them to imagine worlds beyond their experience. Listening to fictional stories helps children to imagine what it feels like to be someone else and to see things from other points of view. The development of these complementary powers of self-knowledge and empathy is crucial in fostering children's ability to make sense of the past.

Stories can be told or read in a range of different languages. As well as stimulating their imagination, listening to stories in their first languages offers bilingual children opportunities to reflect on particular episodes of their lives and to hold on to significant events. This helps to build up enormous resources to draw on when they encounter stories in English.

Stories and history

The National Curriculum recognises that 'pupils should be helped to develop an awareness of the past through stories from different periods and cultures.

Stories can offer children opportunities for:

- ❑ developing oral descriptive and narrative skills
- ❑ drawing out experiences and knowledge in their own language and culture
- ❑ recalling and making sense of their past experiences
- ❑ acquiring the language and conventions of time and place
- ❑ gaining insight into other people's thoughts and emotions (empathy)

❑ identifying similarities and differences between past and present

❑ understanding that events have causes as well as consequences

❑ making judgements about persons and events (interpretation)

❑ realising that pictures and print contain valuable information (evidence)

❑ anticipating sequences and predicting outcomes

❑ imagining different worlds

❑ motivating children to role-play, draw and paint, read and write, make models and constructions

Choosing appropriate stories

The book corner should include a selection of stories suitable for developing early historical concepts and skills. The stories (see chapter seven) might be chosen for a range of reasons, as suggested below:

❑ The story might have potential for stimulating children to recall and talk about their past experiences, to imagine other worlds, eg stories featuring:

— journeys and travel

— grandparents

— babies and children

— home routines

— events which take place over a period of time

— special days and festive occasions

— myths and legends from a variety of cultures.

❑ Stories might be chosen for their specifical historical content, providing knowledge about people in past times, eg stories featuring:

— real people who have contributed to improving our world

— accounts of people's ways of life in different past ages.

❑ The story might positively convey the diversity of people's ways of life in the past and the experiences of both women and men.

❑ T.he illustrations might be strong and positive, helping children to interpret the events in the pictures.

❑ The story might be available in children's first languages.

Stories as mini-topics

As suggested in chapter two, stories are an essential dimension of the topic-based curriculum. Expanded into mini- topics, they can provide children with new directions to explore.

Stories can be used at key moments in the course of the topic. You might consider starting the school day with a story. This may well motivate the children in their follow-up activities, as children tend to carry the excitement of a good story into other learning contexts.

The value of stories in fostering historical attitudes, concepts and skills depends rather more on follow-up discussion and activities than on the simple telling of the tale. Opportunities for children to revisit stories are therefore crucial. The story-webs on the following pages illustrate what might be done with some favourite story books.

Classification of story: Which aspects are real and which are fantasy? Discuss how the story alternates between past and present
History, Geography, English AT1

Discussion of story: What are some of the things grandma has seen and in which countries? When did she see them? Why does she tell Madeleine about her wonderful experiences? How does she describe Madeleine? Discuss thoughts and feelings.
History, English AT 1, Geography

The book's fine illustrations make it particularly appropriate to tell the story using only the pictures, discussing the rich detail in each (various elements, colours, mood, sequence. time, place). Ask the children to identify their favourite picture, draw or paint it and write about it.
Art, AT1 History, English AT1, Geography

Draw and write about a visit to or from grandma, or an outing (real or imaginary) with her. Sequence Madeleine's grandma's memories on a time-line.
Art AT 1, English AT 3, History, IT AT 1

WHEN GRANDMA CAME

Organise a grandmas' morning/afternoon in school, with refreshments. Encourage grandparents to come into the classroom throughout the year and talk about, how and where they used to travel when they were little. Also try to collect pictures and artefacts of the time. *History, English AT1*

Graph work: ask some children to carry out a classroom survey to find out the ages of the children's grandmas, how many were born and/or live locally, how many elsewhere in Britain, or in another country...?
Maths ATs 1-2, Geography, IT AT 1-2

Relate to children's own experiences: When does their grandma visit? What does she say and do? Where does she live? Do they visit her? When was the last time they did so? How do they feel when they see her? Does their grandma look like Madeleine's grandma? Is she younger or older?
History, English AT1 Geography

Try to get the story taped and translated into different languages. Parents or grandparents could use the pictures to tell the story in their own language. *Cross-curricular*

STORY WEB 1: *When Grandma Came* by Jill Paton Walsh and Sophy Williams, Penguin Viking 1992.

Classification of story: real people or fictional characters? Where might the story be set? When might it have happened? How can we guess (picture clues)? Discuss the contrast in the story between real and imagined events.
History, English AT1 Geography

Explore and discuss the names the children use for their grandparents. Have them written and displayed in different languages and scripts.
Education for Citizenship, IT AT 1

Encourage children to investigate some area of interest from the story, eg finding out more about balloon travel. Visit a transport museum, collect pictures of former means of transport. Compare travelling when grandpa was a child with today.
History, Geography, English ATs 1-2, Science A T 3

Ask children to sequence the balloon's journey orally and by drawing/writing a time-line. Encourage them to talk about familiar places in terms of journeys, distance and direction. Get them to record weather observations over a period of time.
History, English ATs 1, 3, Geography, IT AT1

A BALLOON
FOR GRANDAD

Visual appreciation: Retell the story through the pictures only, discussing the rich detail of the images. Ask the children to identify their favourite picture, draw or paint it and write about it. Have the story taped in different languages (parents could do this from the pictures). Encourage children to go back to the story.
Cross-curricular

Relate to children's own experiences: Where do they live? Where does grandpa live? Does he look like Abdulla? Is he younger or older? When did they last speak to/write to/ visit grandpa? How did they travel? How long did it take them?
History, Geography, English AT 1

Provide props for children to role-play the characters and imaginatively extend the story. Could another story be developed from Abdulla's point of view...?
English AT 1, History

Discuss the story: What is it about? What about thoughts and feelings of characters; why does Sam cry? What does his dad say then? Discuss the sequences of the balloon's journey: similarities and differences, eg between where Sam lives and where his grandpa lives.
History, English AT 1 , Geography

STORY WEB 2: *A Balloon for Grandad* by Nigel Gray and June Ray, Collins Picture Lions 1988

Discussion of story: What did Ben want for his next birthday? What did his mum say to him? What did he see on the screen? Why did he want to have two kites? Why was he taken to the museum? When was his baby brother born? When did he come home? What did Ben give him? Why was Ben feeling proud at school?
English AT 1, History

Visual appreciation: Discuss the events in the story pictures, ask children to identify their favourite picture, to draw/paint, and write about it.
History, Art AT2, English ATs 1, 3

Relate to children's own experiences — birthdays, siblings, presents, toys. How far back can they remember their birthdays? Can they remember when their little brother/sister was born? Did he/she look like Ben's baby? Can they remember when they got their favourite toy? Have they ever been to a museum? What can they remember about it?
History, English, AT 1

Sequence the events in the story.
Using pictures as evidence, discuss the changes brought by the different seasons. Relate to children's own growth and development (children could bring in two or three photos showing how they have grown).
History, Geography, English A T 1

BEN'S BABY

Have the story read and discussed in another appropriate language (eg Chinese). Approach parents to tape-record the story in other languages.
Collect and sing songs and tell stories about the different seasons.
Cross-curricular

Ask children to bring in their favourite old toy. Discuss emotional value, memories. Compare 'oldness', design, physical features, and construction.
History, English AT 1, Science AT2

Design, construct and fly a kite with the children. Collect and display items, foods, objects, artefacts etc associated with different seasons or festivals. *Cross-curricular, esp Design/Tech ATs 1, 2*

Classification of story: Real people or fiction? Discussion: When and where might the story have happened (picture clues)? Time-line: Over what period of time does the story take place?
History, Geography, English AT 1

STORY WEB 3: *Ben's Baby* by Michael Foreman, Magi Publications 1989. Available in Vietnamese, Chinese, Greek, Urdu, Bengali, Gujarati, Panjabi, Hindi

Classification of story: real people or fictional? Discussion: Where is the story set? When does it take place? Are we given any clues?
History, Geography, English AT 1

Encourage parents/grandparents to come in and share their knowledge of the Caribbean by cooking, playing a musical instrument, story-telling or describing a childhood experience. *Cross-curricular*

Relate to children's own holidays/trips/hobbies/home experiences: Have any children been to, or heard stories about, the Caribbean? Have they heard a steel band? When? Have they been to a market, to the sea-side..? Did it look like the market scene in the story? Where else have they been? What can they remember? Does their grandma look like the grandma in the story?
English AT 1, Geography, History

Make a collection of artefacts, pictures, musical instruments, fruits.. originating from the Caribbean. Discuss physical features, design, function, taste.. Sort into sets (eg new, old, by shape, size, colour..)
Cross-curricular

ONE
SMILING
GRANDMA

Discussion of story: What are the different things that the little girl sees and does on her holiday? How many things does she see? What does she do when she sees them? How does she feel? Can children remember and put in the right sequence the different things she sees? What do they like about the story?
English ATs 1-2, Maths AT2, History

Visual appreciation: Discuss various aspects of the story pictures: events, mood, use of colour. Children could also draw, paint or write about their favourite picture.
Art ATs 1-2, English ATs 1, 3, IT, AT 1

Sing songs and rhymes from the Caribbean. Make up and sing other simple counting songs with the children.
Music ATs 1-2, Maths AT 1-2

Visit places and events celebrating Caribbean traditions (eg Carnival at the Commonwealth Institute, London and Bradford). Compare weather, plant and bird life in Britain and the Caribbean
Cross-curricular, esp. Geography, Education for Citizenship

STORY WEB 4: *One Smiling Grandma* by Ann Marie Linden and Lynne Russell. William Heinemann 1992

Classification of story: Real people or fictional characters? Discuss where the story might be set. In what country? Did it happen recently, a long time ago, a very long time ago? How can we guess (picture clues)?
History, Geography, English AT1

Discussion of story: Compare the children's ideas with the teacher's. Talk about the importance of remembering and imagining. Emphasise the children's cleverness in knowing about other places and countries. Ask children to identify sequences set in the present and those set in the past.
History, English AT 1

Relate to children's own experiences: When and where did they last go on holiday? How long ago? How did they travel? Discuss similarities and differences between their holiday experiences and those of the children in the story. What can they remember? What did they bring back? Bring out and discuss children's own ideas about what 'magic' is.
History, Geography, English AT 1

Ask children to bring in photos of their holidays and/or items of interest from another place. In small groups, discuss the pictures with the children. Ask children to sequence their holidays on a time-line (see below*) and to classify the items in terms of place of origin.
History, Geography, English AT1

DO YOU BELIEVE IN MAGIC ?

Encourage parents to come in and write about their child's holiday — the child could draw the pictures. Ask a parent or other adult to talk to the children about a 'magical' holiday experience from their childhood.
History, Geography, English AT1, 3, IT AT 1

*eg 'holidays I went on after I started school/holidays I went on before I started school', starting with the recent past and working backwards.

Visit the seaside to observe the scene, listen to the sounds of the sea, collect shells, pebbles.. Or a Maritime Museum (eg the Cutty Sark) to look at different kinds of sea transport and the changes over the past 100 years.
History, Geography, Science ATs 3-4

Visual appreciation: Discuss the events in the story pictures and ask the children to identity their favourite image, draw it and write about it. Discuss the idea that people remember different things from the past. Get the children to recall a recent shared experience (eg a visit) and compare their memories.
Art A T 1-2, English ATs 1, 3, History

Retell the story in another appropriate language, in small groups and as a whole class activity. Encourage the children to verbalise their knowledge of the two languages and the similarities and differences between them.
English AT1, Education for Citizenship

STORY WEB 5: *Do You Believe in Magic?* by Saviour Pirotta and Mrinal Mitra, Mantra Publishing Limited. 1991. Available in Arabic, Bengali, Chinese, Gujarati, Urdu

Classification of story: real people or fiction? Discussion: Where might the story be set? When might it have happened? What clues are we given? Time-line: How long do events take (a day, a week, a month..)?
History, English AT 1, Geography

Put together a collection of home objects and ask the children to sort them into different rooms. Visits: suitable museums to look at rooms in the past (eg The Open Hearth Kitchen and The 1930s rooms at the Geffrye Museum, York Museum of History.)
Cross-curricular

Discussion of story: Who lives in the house? What happens on Saturdays? What was the 'terrible thing' that happened a few days ago? What did mum decide to do when she discovered the mess? What did the children do then? What did they have to eat? How long did mum do nothing? Why did 'frog' say a prayer? What did the children promise? What did they learn?
History, English AT 1

Set up a 'changing kitchen' in the classroom. What would the children put in it? Explore a range of ingredients, foods and packagings. Encourage children to set up an attractive library space: Which books would they display?
Design/Tech AT 1, Maths A T 3

MUM'S STRIKE

Relate to children's own home routines: How do they spend Saturdays? What do they like doing? Can they remember what they did last Saturday, the Saturday before...? Do they make a mess? Who does the tidying up? Has their mum ever done anything like the mum in the story? Do they pray? On which days and where?
History, English AT 1

Visual appreciation: discuss the events in the pictures. Ask children to identify their favourite image, draw/paint and write about it; and draw their favourite room/living space at home and write about it.
English ATs 1, 3, Art AT 1, 2, Geography

Children can talk about their favourite room or 'living space' and what makes it special. Use images to identify differences in room size, materials, furniture, interior designs; and identify changes in rooms between the present and the past
Cross-curricular, esp. History

Explore the motives, behaviour and feelings of the characters in the story. Discuss the different points of view: the mum's, the children's. Retell the story in another language as a whole class activity and in small groups. Encourage children to verbalise their knowledge of the two languages — the similarities and differences between them.
History, English AT 1, Education for Citizenship

STORY WEB 6: *Mum's Strike* by Marieluise Ritter, Magi Publications 1989. Available in Gujarati, Panjabi, Urdu, Bengali

Classification of story: real people or fiction? Discussion: Where is the story set? When do events happen (nowadays, a long time ago, a very long time ago)? How can we guess? (picture and language clues)
History, Geography, English AT 1

Relate to children's own experiences: Have they ever lived in/been to a village? How long ago? Can they talk about it, describe its smells, colours, climate etc? Talk about the streets where they live now (homes, shops, people, places of worship, sounds, smells etc): the foods and fruit that they eat at home. Discuss changes in their own lives.
History, Geography

Discussion of story: What is the story about? How is the bird able to see so many things? Why does the bird want to find out about his past lives? How can the palmist tell the past? Talk about different belief systems (eg that some people believe in a previous and an after life). Talk about changes associated with the passage of time: and about people, living creatures, animals who have no fixed home.
History, Religious Education, English AT 1

Collect images of places that are familiar to the children. Discuss, in small groups, the pictures with the children, bringing out similarities and differences between, eg, village life and town life.
History, Geography, English AT 1, Art ATs 1, 2

THE BIRD WHO WAS AN ELEPHANT

Retell the story in another language in small groups and as a whole class activity. Encourage children to verbalise their knowledge of the two languages — the similarities and differences between them.
English, A T 1. Education for Citizenship

Encourage parents to come and help groups of children make some of the food in the story: samosas, bhajias, chapatis and perhaps bring in and talk about some of the spices and ingredients used in Indian cooking.
Cross-curricular, Education for citizenship

Visits: identify some aspect of the local environment for children to explore the idea of how places change: aspects of the school itself, the contrast between an old and a new building in the neighbourhood, or observing changes arising from the redevelopment of a particular site.
History, Geography, Science A T 3

Visual appreciation: discuss various aspects of the story pictures: events, mood, use of colour, etc. Children could also draw, paint or write about their favourite image (or a particular aspect of it).
Cross-curricular, esp. Art ATs 1-2

STORY WEB 7: *The Bird Who Was an Elephant* by Aleph Kamal and Frane Lessac, Cambridge University Press 1989. Available in Panjabi, Gujarati, Benaali, Urdu

The function and importance of trees as providers of air, water, shade, shelter, clothes, medicines, fruits, flowers. Conservation and recycling: provide examples of things which can be used again rather than thrown away after first use. What can we do to improve our home, school, local environment?
Science ATs 2, 3 , Geography, English AT 1

Classification of story: What is a folktale? Discussion: Where is the story set? When did the events happen? How do we know? Time-line: How long is the story (does it happen over a day, a week, a month, several years..)? 'In long-ago India, when warrior princes ruled the land..' Fact or point of view?
History, English, A T 1

Relate to children's own experiences: Have they ever been anywhere where people look and dress like Amrita? Have they ever been in a storm? Where have they seen trees? Can they describe them? Have they noticed any special qualities about trees? What do they think trees are used for? How many things made from trees can they find in the classroom and in their home?
Geography History, Science ATs 2, 3, English AT 1

Discussion of story: Why did Amrita love the trees? Why were they so important to her? Why did the Maharajah (king) want to cut down the trees? How did Amrita feel when her favourite tree was chopped down? How did the people prevent all the other trees from being cut down? Why was the Maharajah angry? What did he do? Why did he decide in the end not to cut the trees down?
History, English AT 1, Geography

THE PEOPLE WHO HUGGED THE TREES

Indian wood block printing/leaf printing Collages and mobiles using tree-based materials eg paper, leaves, twigs, seeds. Making tree-dressing decorations. Role-play based on characters and events in the story.
Art ATs 1-2, English AT 1, Design/Tech ATs 2, History

Visits: explore the school environment and/or local woodland. Each child could adopt a chosen tree and observe, describe, measure it over a period of time. The properties and uses of wood as a material.
Science A T 3, Maths AT 3, Geography, English AT 1

Weather and seasons in the Indian sub-continent: compare with Britain. Children can describe the different kinds of weather they know, and role-play, paint or write about how they might feel if they were in a storm.
Geography, Science A T 4, English AT 1

Visual appreciation: discuss the events in the pictures, ask children to draw and write about their favourite picture. Tell other stories based on folktales from around the world.
Cross-curricular

STORY WEB 8: *The People Who Hugged the Trees* by Deborah Lee Rose and Birgitta Saflund, Robert Rinehart International 1990

Chapter four

Remembering the past:
personal memories and family narratives

a. Personal Time-Lines

As suggested in the previous chapter, relating what happens in stories to their own experience helps children develop the ability to sort out the order in which events occurred. Their personal memories can be sketched out in the form of timelines, enabling children to recall and represent their own past through a sequence of time stretching backwards from the present. In moving from the imaginative world of stories to their real life experience, children will also:

❏ begin to see their personal histories within a wider context of real events in the world

❏ develop a deeper understanding about the passage of time

❏ begin to understand differences between longer and shorter measures of time

It might be helpful to begin by talking about different measures of time — morning, afternoon, evening, night, days, weeks, months, seasons, years. This can be linked to a recent period of activities shared by the whole class or to a number of public celebrations (Diwali, Christmas, Chinese New Year), encouraging the children to talk about their recollections of these events in their correct sequence.

Next, extend the discussion to the children's memories of significant events and occasions in their life over a longer period. Parents can be invited into the classroom to help their child recall shared family experiences and occasions.

A first time-line can be quite simple. Children can draw or write their recollection of specific events before and after they started school, with adults acting as scribes, and then attempt to sequence them in the correct order. Parents might contribute photographs or artefacts to add to their child's personal history.

Although it is not essential to indicate measures of time passed at this stage, it might be useful to encourage children to begin to use time phrases such as 'when I was four.'

'Washing lines', complete with string and clothes pegs, are an eye-catching device for displaying time-lines in the classroom. Children are usually very eager to hang their pictures on the washing line and can move them around when the discovery of fresh information warrants a change in the sequencing order.

As children develop greater understanding of the nature of time, they can recall and sequence events outside their personal histories — favourite television programmes, seasonal changes, events in the local neighbourhood, for instance.

b. Interviewing parents

Seeking out information from parents about their lives helps children to move a little further into the past. Moreover, by learning to use a tape recorder to record their conversations, children begin to develop oral historical skills, ie techniques of gathering evidence about the past from the spoken word.

It is important to prepare the ground carefully. Let the parents know by informal word and/or letter why their children will be interviewing them and the significance of the project.

Researching children's families is a sensitive issue. Some of the points made in chapter one about working with parents might usefully be referred to again. Some children might not be able to collect family-based information and will need to be given alternative people to 'adopt' and find out about (eg the teacher's or head's family, a carer, another adult connected with the school, an acquaintance from the local community).

The interview questions may well be suggested by the topic itself, but it is advisable to draw up a final list after discussions with the children. Give them some advance preparation of tape-recording an interview (eg with other children, the teacher, other adults in school).

As part of their work on *Homes*, for instance, children could converse with their parents in their first language, asking questions such as:

- ❏ When were you born?
- ❏ Where were you born?
- ❏ Can you remember the first home you lived in?
- ❏ Was it like the home we live in now?
- ❏ When did you come to live in this house?
- ❏ Where did you live before?
- ❏ Have you kept any old things or pictures that I can show my teacher and friends in school?
- ❏ How long have we lived here?
- ❏ When do we celebrate special occasions at home?
- ❏ Is there another place you think of as home?

This can lead to some interesting follow-up activities. The teacher, with the assistance of a bilingual adult if necessary, might work with a group of children, including the interviewer. The recording can be supported by visual evidence, such as photographs or artefacts brought in by the child or assembled by the teacher. Have as many visual clues as possible at hand to support the group discussion.

The children can be encouraged to talk about the interview: who took part, when did it take place, did they have to stop and continue later..? From the contents of the interview, the adults can initiate a discussion focusing on a particular aspect, eg 'how does the home you live in now differ from the home your mum or dad lived in when they were little?'

The teacher can encourage the children to contribute their thoughts and experiences by identifying the key moments of the conversation and the accompanying visual clues.

It might also be possible to develop a time-line by putting extracts from the recording into their correct time sequence. The information from the interview and visual evidence can also be a stimulus for written work, for example, 'things that happened when Salma's mum was a little girl' .

c. Grandparents

Grandparents' accounts of their memories of the past — their own experiences or events they have witnessed — can take children back a stage further. Inviting grandparents into the classroom is a way of valuing children's membership of a specific family and community; it might also give the grandparents a new sense of worth, a new significance to their lives.

The value of a good story coming from someone who is known to the children cannot be over-emphasised. Again, however, this needs careful preparation: a grandparents' open day, as suggested in story-web 1, informal chats with parents, letters of invitation to selected grandparents.

Select them according to the chosen topic and whether they have clear memories of a particular experience in their life history —

eg living on a certain street in the locality during the second world war (topics: *Homes, Our Community*), or moving from the Indian subcontinent or the Caribbean to Britain in the 1950s (topics: *Journeys, Families*).

A discussion session with the children before the grandparents' visit will establish the kinds of questions they would like to ask. Once again, as much visual evidence as possible should be at hand to complement the narration. After the visit the children can write about the things they remember from the talk.

Children who have grandparents living far away in Britain or in another country, can be encouraged, with the help of parents, to write and ask the following:

- ❑ What is your name?
- ❑ When were you born?
- ❑ What country were you born in?
- ❑ Did you go to school?
- ❑ How long did it take you each day?
- ❑ How did you travel?
- ❑ What did you do in class?
- ❑ What games did you play?
- ❑ If you were not at school, how did you spend the day?
- ❑ Please could you send me any photos, pictures or things from when you were little like me?

The replies might take some time to arrive but are usually well worth waiting for. Through discussion, children will be able to compare their experiences of school with those of their grandma or grandpa at the same age. They can reflect on and begin to identify differences not only between past and present times, but also between the recent past of parents and the more distant past of grandparents.

Picturing the past: images

The importance of the visual dimension has already been demonstrated. Images are a highly effective resource for getting children who are just beginning to read to talk and learn about the past.

Children are surrounded by visual images in their everyday lives. Nurturing their ability to see and observe might well be as important as teaching them reading, writing and counting. Visual literacy skills play a crucial role in developing modes of imagination which privilege artistic, literary and historical creativity.

Visual images and National Curriculum History

National Curriculum history recognises the importance of images. Children, it is suggested, should be able to:

☐ talk about what they see in an old photograph

☐ put a series of personal and family photographs and belongings in chronological order

☐ use information from old newspapers, photographs and maps to describe life in a local street in the 1930s.

A crucial historical source

Images offer all children:

☐ opportunities to talk about their own experiences of the past, of different places and countries

☐ an authentic source for comparing past and present and for different interpretations

☐ information and knowledge about people, places and events

- stimulus for the development of the powers of reasoning, questioning, predicting
- opportunities for discussing what can and cannot be learnt from the picture (incompleteness of evidence)
- motivation for historical drawing, painting, writing
- opportunities for comparing similarities and differences between different kinds of visual images (photographs, paintings, packagings)
- a resource for affirming cultural diversity.

Bilingual children

Images offer children who are potentially bilingual the opportunity to develop their skills through discussion with other children and adults with whom they share a first language. In co-operative group activities, pair off children who share a language, especially where a more fluent child can support the learning of the less fluent child.

A cross-curricular resource

Pictures are also valuable in other areas of the National Curriculum. For instance, children might:

- identify different kinds of art, present and past and look at and talk about examples of the work of well-known artists from a variety of periods and cultures (*Art*)
- use words and pictures to describe their observations and experiences of the weather and seasons (*Geography*)
- look at and talk about pictures, maps and photographs of homes and villages, towns and cities, in different parts of the world (*Geography*)
- use talk, pictures, drawings, models to develop their design proposals (*Design/Technology*)
- create pictures and patterns using 2-D shapes or 3-D objects (*Mathematics*).

Collecting images

Most schools and teachers collect a range of visual materials — posters, postcards, photographs, advertising images. Museums (see chapter nine) are the best source for images of the past. They house good collections of reasonably priced posters and postcard-size pictures including black-and-white photographs and colour paintings. Local history groups, library and leisure services also produce pictorial records of local life in the past. We have noted how parents, grandparents, teachers and older adults in the community might also be able to contribute.

Contemporary visuals can be built up from magazines such as *Child Education*, travel brochures, regional and national tourist offices; from purchases at card and poster shops and art galleries.

Some of the larger visuals can be displayed in the classroom and discussed with the children. It is particularly interesting to juxtapose a contemporary image with a picture of the past.

Modern day postcards and photographs can be used alongside the pictures featured in this book to compare present and past.

The pictures in this book

Ten pictures are featured: six photographs and four paintings (see pages 35-44).

The photographs

❶ A woman porter assisting a passenger on the Chancery Lane underground platform London, 1940. Women were first employed by the Underground as porters at this station in September 1940 during the Second World War.

❷ Children boarding a District Line train at Ravenscourt Park, west London, for a day's outing to Eastcote near Harrow, July 1934.

③ Charing Cross Hotel in central London and the Strand traffic, July 1923.

④ Women cleaning a bus at the London General Omnibus Company's Willesden garage, London, during the First World War.

⑤ Indian Suffragettes demonstrating during the Coronation Procession of June 1911.

⑥ Suffragette leader Christabel Pankhurst addressing a crowd in Trafalgar Square, London 1908.

The paintings

⑦ St. Pancras Hotel and Station from Pentonville Road: Sunset, by John O'Connor, 1884. St. Pancras Hotel, built in 1867-76, was one of the major Gothic buildings in London. Notice also the postman opening the pillarbox, a number of sandwich-board men, horse-drawn buses and trams and a hansom cab. The viewpoint is a rooftop on the corner of Rodney Street and Pentonville Road. The full colour original is featured on the front cover of this book.

⑧ Upper Lisson Street, Paddington, from Chapel Street, about 1837. Upper Lisson and Chapel Streets were mainly shopping streets and here a small crowd has gathered to watch a Jack-in-the-Green (chimney sweep) procession, which can be seen in centre foreground. A number of boy chimney sweeps are collecting money.

⑨ A mounted prince begging water from four women at a well, somewhere in north India, about 1720. The full colour original is featured on the back cover of this book.

⑩ Miriam Makani, mother of the Mughal Indian king, Akbar, travelling by river boat, late sixteenth century.

Children's perceptions

Pictures appeal powerfully to children's acute powers of observation, enabling them to engage directly with the past and respond to the evidence in front of them.

Children generally use two main strategies to help them make sense of pictures: they look for clues, elements with which they are familiar, something within their personal or cultural experience; and they try to interpret what is happening in the image.

The featured pictures are designed to build on children's previous experience of visuals, both in informal everyday contexts and in relation to some of the activities suggested earlier in the book.

All the pictures contain a wealth of detail about people doing all kinds of things, and all have elements which will attract children's interest and curiosity. And each picture tells a story.

The photographs and paintings can also contribute to widening children's perceptions of the range of people who played important historical roles through the ages.

Activities

Initially, show the class a few large pictures and discuss them with the whole class.

This can be followed up with more in-depth sessions in small groups. If possible include adults in the groups who share the children's first languages.

Talking about pictures

The children can start by simply talking about what they see in one or two of the pictures provided. They can be given prompts to focus and animate their thinking, eg

> '...I'm not quite sure what is happening here.. Can you help?' or

> '...Does this picture make you think of anything? Can you tell me about it?'

Allowing children the freedom to speculate about what they see and understand in the pictures helps them to take risks, exchange ideas and learn from each other's thoughts.

Then and now

Next, introduce some contemporary postcards or photographs to stimulate a simple comparison between present and past or new and old. Invite the children to compare two pictures, asking them:

❑ What can you see in the pictures?

❑ What do you think is happening?

❑ Does anything in the pictures remind you of something?

❑ Where do you think the pictures were taken (..locally, somewhere else in Britain, in another country..)?

❑ When do you think the pictures were taken (..nowadays, a long time ago..)?

❑ Which one do you think is new and which one is old?

❑ What kind of pictures (..photograph, painting..) do you think these are?

❑ Also ask questions about specific aspects of each picture.

Different points of view

Give a small group of children one of the pictures and ask them to write the story they think it tells. Their versions can be compared and discussed with the whole class.

Differences between times in the past

As children acquire greater experience of reading pictures, they can be given progressively more sophisticated tasks.

Lay out half a dozen pictures, preferably a mix of black-and-white and colour, on the floor in a quiet area of the classroom. Ask the children, working in pairs, to pick out a picture which they think is new (about now), an old one (about a long time ago) and a very old one (about a very long time ago). They could discuss and agree their choice and report back to the teacher.

It might be interesting to get children to compare photographs with paintings and to work through commonly held assumptions by which we associate black-and-white with old and colour with new.

Changes

Teachers might take their own photographs of, for instance, present-day Charing Cross Hotel or the speakers' rostrum in Trafalgar Square during a public meeting. Children can compare the contemporary photographs with the historical ones and try to work out what has changed and what has not.

Revisiting

At this stage, getting the picture right (ie historically accurate) is less important than the confidence to ask questions, speculate and hypothesise about possible alternatives. Children's historical statements are bound to be tentative and provisional. So it is important to give them frequent opportunities to revisit the pictures in the light of their developing visual literacy.

❶ *A woman porter assisting a passenger on the Chancery Lane underground platform, London, 1940. Women were first employed by the Underground as porters at this station in September 1940 during the Second World War.*
(Museum of London)

❷ *Children boarding a District Line train at Ravenscourt Park, west London, for a day's outing to Eastcote near Harrow, July 1934.*

(Museum of London)

❸ *Charing Cross Hotel in central London and the Strand traffic, July 1923.*

(Museum of London)

❹ *Women cleaning a bus at the London General Omnibus Company's Willesden garage, London, during the First World War.*

(Museum of London)

❺ *Indian Suffragettes demonstrating during the Coronation Procession of June 1911.*

(Museum of London)

❺ *Suffragette leader Christabel Pankhurst addressing a crowd in Trafalgar Square, London 1908.*

(Museum of London)

❼ *St. Pancras Hotel and Station from Pentonville Road: Sunset, by John O'Connor, 1884. St. Pancras Hotel, built in 1867-76, was one of the major Gothic buildings in London. Notice also the postman opening the pillarbox, a number of sandwich-board men, horse-drawn buses and trams and a hansom cab. The viewpoint is a rooftop on the corner of Rodney Street and Pentonville Road. The full colour original is featured on the front cover of this book.*

(Museum of London)

❽ *Upper Lisson Street, Paddington, from Chapel Street, about 1837. Upper Lisson and Chapel Streets were mainly shopping streets and here a small crowd has gathered to watch a Jack-in-the-Green (chimney sweep) procession, which can be seen in centre foreground. A number of boy chimney sweeps are collecting money.*

(Museum of London)

❾ *A mounted prince begging water from four women at a well, somewhere in north India, about 1720. The full colour original is featured on the back cover of this book.*

(Victoria & Albert Museum)

❿ *Miriam Makani, mother of the Mughal Indian king, Akbar, travelling by river boat, late sixteenth century.*

(Victoria & Albert Museum)

Chapter six

Experiencing the past: artefacts and visits

Artefacts are real things made by people. Like visual images, they are part of children's everyday lives. In their homes and communities, children have already observed, examined, handled and preserved objects. Some of these might well be cultural artefacts handed down over generations, originating from a particular region or religious tradition.

As a multi-sensory learning resource, artefacts have a rare capacity to engage children's curiosity and interest to want to know more. They offer another ideal context for supporting the development of bilingual literacy.

Artefacts and history

The National Curriculum recognises artefacts as one of the main sources of historical knowledge. As material remains of the past,

they help stimulate children's appreciation of the role of things in their own lives and in past times.

By working with real objects, handling, discussing, remembering and making comparisons, children can begin to understand:

☐ the physical effects of time on things made by humans

☐ an object's 'feeling of age' compared to the newness of a reproduction; and the concept of an original

☐ a variety of materials and what they were used for

☐ how people perceived the world in which they lived

☐ differences and similarities between our needs today and those of people in the past

☐ similarities and differences in cultural values.

Artefacts past and present

❏ Many objects that in Britain are regarded as belonging to the past may still be in everyday use in many parts of the world. Some children might for instance have seen lanterns or bicycles made in what would be considered outdated technologies in the West still in use on the streets of Bangladesh or Vietnam.

❏ When discussing artefacts, it is important to avoidconveying messages of inferiority and superiority related to old and new. By adopting a global perspective, we can emphasise that people in many parts of the world still find certain things that we have discarded perfectly suitable for their needs.

Handling artefacts

a. The Suitcase

A school can build up a temporary collection of artefacts by borrowing items from parents and grandparents, teachers and other adults in the school and from local community organisations. Jumble sales, junk and second-hand shops are often remarkably useful places for additional material.

An exciting way of introducing children to working with artefacts is through a suitcase type activity, particularly if its contents are made up of borrowings from local sources known to the children: the parents, grandparents, adults in the school.

Exploring the contents of an old suitcase containing a range of artefacts and memorabilia will stimulate children to discuss and hypothesise about:

❏ the feeling of age of the various artefacts (new, old, or very old... used nowadays, when my mum was a little girl, or when my grandma was a little girl?)

❏ what they might have been used for.. (does this remind you of anything that we use today?)

❏ the identity of the owner of the suitcase.. (was the person young or old, male or female, English, Scottish, Irish, Welsh, Indian, Chinese, Caribbean..?)

❏ where the traveller might be coming from

❏ why she or he might be carrying these items.. (people carry what is important to them — aspects of their history — when they move from one place to another)

❏ what can be known for certain from the evidence, and what is merely surmise.

The contents of the (preferably old and worn-looking) suitcase need to provide clues to help children to build up a picture of its owner. Alongside the artefacts, add a few contemporary items (eg travel tickets, presents and personal belongings the traveller might be carrying).

The suitcase could include old postcards or letters, photographs, articles of clothing, books, toys/games, coins, newspapers/magazines, musical instruments, crafts, small tins or boxes.

b. The Treasure Chest

Various educational sources lend out artefact boxes specifically for teaching and learning in the classroom. Museums (check with the education department at your nearest museum), library services, teachers' centres, often provide ready-to-use collections on specific topics.

The *Commonwealth Institute*, based in London and Bradford, has produced five boxes of artefacts on toys, homes, festivals, hats and appropriate technology. The items include dolls, puppets and recycled toys, bowls, pots and baskets, tools, lamps and a model bicycle. They originate from several parts of the world including Britain, the Indian sub-continent, West Africa and the Caribbean.

Arranged into 'treasure chests', the artefacts appeal immediately to children's sense of curiosity and are ideal for small group work in the classroom.

Although the items are examples of things currently in use around the world, remember that many bilingual children may be able to relate them to aspects of their past experience: objects they know and can talk about as a result of living in or visiting a particular country; or things they are familiar with through their family's cultural traditions.

The treasure chest is a variation on the suitcase activity but without the supporting clues relating to the traveller. The children can investigate the artefacts directly, guided by the following questions:

❑ What does it look like?
❑ What does it feel like?
❑ What colour is it?
❑ What shape is it?
❑ Is it decorated? How?
❑ Does it have any writing on it? Do you know what it says and in which language?
❑ What is it made of?
❑ What was it used for?
❑ Does it remind you of anything?
❑ How does it make you feel? Do you like it?
❑ Does it look new or old?
❑ Can you think of any advantages (eg cost, environmental..) or disadvantages for people who used it?

Following the discussion, children can draw an artefact of their choice and write a few things about it. The same object can be drawn from different angles, encouraging children to represent size and shape accurately in their drawings so they record their experience of the artefact.

c. The Visit

Visits to appropriate museums provide yet another way for children to investigate artefacts as material remains of the past. An expert input by a museum teacher makes this a particularly valuable experience.

Year 1 class at St. Michael's School, Camden, had already worked through the activities described above as part of their topic on homes. Their visit to the *Museum of London* had been planned to reinforce the learning gains and to introduce the children to a period of the past beyond living memory. A number of parents accompanied the children and their two teachers.

The museum teacher, Emma Webb, conducted a 'spot the difference' teaching session. The children handled and discussed some everyday objects from a century ago: a child's boot, a toy mangle, an iron, a lantern. The purpose was to get the children to hypothesise about who might have used these items and on what occasions and to identify differences between then and now.

d. The Teaching Session

'Has anybody here been to a museum before?' Emma begins. 'Yes, with my mum.. with my dad,' some children answer. 'Why do people come and visit museums? What is there to see in a museum?' continues Emma.
'Because it tells us about olden times.'

'It has things from a long time ago..'

'Maybe people put old things somewhere so that they remain new,' suggests Sara.

'Yes. Very good. Lots and lots of things in a museum are from a long long time ago, further back than you can remember and further back than even I can remember.. These are things which people in olden times, people in the past, used to have.' 'We have things at home that used to belong to my dada,' (paternal grandfather) observes Hameeda.

'Yes... and just like you're wearing shoes and a jumper and those nice earrings.. Maybe in one hundred years time those things will be in a museum and people will go and look at them to try and find out some things about you, about what you used to wear and which part of the world those earrings came from... 'So people come to museums today to look at things that belonged to people a long long time ago, to try and find out different things about them..'

Emma continues:

'Let's look at some things we have here.' She picks up an artefact from the table and shows it to the whole class.

'This would have been in a school a hundred years ago. If a hundred years ago I was your teacher and you were my class, I might have had one of these on my desk.. What do you think this could be? What is it made of?'

'It's made of metal..'

'Yes, it's made of metal.. Is it thick or thin?'

The children hesitate.

'It's difficult to tell, isn't it?' continues the teacher. She passes the object to some children. 'Does it feel heavy or light?'

'Quite light.. very light.'

'What about the points. What do they feel like?'

'Sharp. .'

'Yes, very sharp, aren't they?.. What shape is it? Is it round or square or..?'

'It's like a star..'

'Good. It's a piece of metal that's in the shape of a star.. What am I holding it by? What's that bit at the top there?'

'It's like a hook..'

'Excellent. It's a little ring at the top like a hook. What else do you notice about it? What has it got up here?' 'Writing.. words,' the children respond.

'Good. There's writing on it.. Can all of you see the writing..? All down here and round the back.. Now if I was a teacher in England one hundred years ago, which is a very long time ago, much longer ago than you and much longer ago than me, I might have had one of these on my desk. What do you think I would use it for? Why might I want to give it to one of the children?'

'To draw round it?' suggests Amanda.

'Now that's a really good idea..Well done. It might be to draw around it. But what does it have that would make it difficult to draw round it..? Why couldn't you lay it down completely flat? See, it's got that little hook there that would get in the way, wouldn't it? Now how might you wear it? Would you like to try it on? What's your name?'

'Shumi.'

'Now, if I gave this to Shumi to wear, what would it mean?'

'That you liked her.. that she was very good.'

'Exactly..that she was a star! It would mean that I thought that she was very, very good and a hundred years ago, in school in England, if I was the teacher and she was being really good, Shumi would have got one of these stars.. What do you get in school today if you're being very good and doing really well..?'

'A happy face,' exclaim the children, laughing..

The children then divided into small groups to investigate the boot, toy mangle, iron and lantern. Supervised by an adult, each group looked at one of these objects, discussed it and drew it from observation. The teacher ended the session with a general discussion of the artefacts and the children's work.

The theme of 'one hundred years ago' was developed further in the afternoon. The children visited one of the museum's Victorian galleries where they could look at and discuss displays of things as they were at the turn of the century; a schoolroom, a kitchen, a grocer's shop and a hansom cab. Some children were discussing what they saw in Bengali, both amongst themselves and with parents.

Local history

a. The School

Working collaboratively in groups, children can investigate different aspects of the school itself (buildings, people, furniture, books, toys, record forms) and compile a list of new/young and old. They can report back to the whole class on their findings.

b. The history trail

A history trail can be designed to explore and find out about the local neighbourhood. This can focus on a few streets near the school, particularly where there is much to see (houses, shops, places of worship, a park, footpath, canal).

Children can begin by trying to identify old and new aspects of the neighbourhood. Next, they can find out how the area has changed recently, by looking at old photographs and interviewing people who have lived locally for a long time (parents, elderly members of the community). The local library is usually a good source of pictures of former times.

In the country a history trail can take in the local farm, village, church, houses and cottages. It is essential that the whole class discuss what they have seen and enjoyed afterwards. They can then record their experiences, drawing a series of pictures and writing captions; writing about what they have seen in the language of time and place, so using terms like 'before', 'after', 'then' and 'now', 'outside' and 'above'; and making a map or chart.

Chapter seven

Assessing children's achievements

Everyday assessments

Opportunities for informally assessing children's achievements arise naturally in everyday classroom interaction. Assessments can be either:

formative, ie to determine whether a child needs more experience of an activity (or different kinds of activities) in order to understand a particular concept or improve a particular skill; or

summative, ie to find out the gains a child has made after exposure to a range of opportunities designed to develop and consolidate learning.

These aspects complement one another and support the delivery of a 'spiral curriculum' in which activities are encountered and revisited at increasing levels of sophistication throughout the key stage.

In planning summative assessments the following suggestions might be useful:

❑ teachers should ensure that children are ready to be assessed

❑ the varied experiences and backgrounds of the children should be taken into account when selecting stories, photographs, pictures, artefacts and objects for assessment

❑ teachers should be in command of a story before they present it to the children

❑ the stories should be told in the teacher's own words rather than simply read out

- teachers should bear in mind that children might achieve at more than one level
- the same level of achievement could be demonstrated through different historical sources

The Level Descriptions

As a result of the Dearing Review of the National Curriculum, level descriptions (LDs) have replaced the former statements of attainment. The Review recognises that in History most children will be working at Levels 1-3 by the end of Key Stage 1.

Level 1

Pupils show awareness of the distinction between present and past in their own and other people's lives. They know and recount episodes from stories about the past. Their developing sense of chronology is shown by their ability to sequence events and objects and to use everyday terms about the passing of time. They are aware that they can find out about the past from sources of information.

Level 2

Pupils demonstrate factual knowledge of aspects of a time beyond living memory, and the personalities and events they have been taught about. Their sense of chronology is shown by their use of terms concerned with the passing of time to order events and objects, and by their ability to make distinctions between aspects of their own lives and past times.

They suggest reasons why people in the past acted as they did. They are beginning to show awareness that the past is represented in different ways and to answer questions about the past using sources of information

Level 3

Pupils demonstrate factual knowledge of a few of the events, people and periods from the appropriate programme of study. Their increasing understanding of chronology is shown through their awareness that the past can be divided into different periods of time, and their recognition of some similarities and differences between these periods. They begin to identify reasons and results. They know that the past is represented in different ways and select information from sources to answer specific questions about the past.

(School Curriculum and Assessment Authority, *History in the National Curriculum*. DFE 1994, p. 14.)

Comment: the level descriptions are meant to assess children's achievements in relation to the full programme of study, rather than in terms of particular strands as in the previous statements of attainment. They are designed to assist the process of summative assessments at the end of the key stage. There is, however, a concern that such an emphasis on summative performance alone might obscure the formative processes which ensure that children are given plenty of opportunities to develop historical concepts and skills.

Evidence of children's achievements

The activities in this book are designed to enable this kind of progression and to allow children the freedom and enjoyment to learn at their own pace. They also offer a range of assessment opportunities as follows:

1. Stories

Teachers may wish to find out whether children can:

(a) place in sequence events in a story about the past. (LD 1)

Evidence of achievement: The child orally recounts episodes from, eg, *Grandfather's Pencil*, *The Toymaker*, or *Our House* in their correct sequence. Alternatively, children draw a few events from a story and write sequenced captions in their first language.

Comment: It is sequencing that is important at this level rather than chronology. It is not essential that the story be about famous people in the past and children are likely to find fictional stories more interesting.

(b) understand that stories may be about real people or fictional characters (LD 1)

Evidence of achievement: The child is able to make out whether or not a story is about a real person or people; and can indicate which, out of a range of stories, are about real people and which are about fictional characters.

Comment: It is important that the stories themselves provide clues as to whether they are real or imaginary. Unlike fictional characters, real people leave material traces of their existence: photographs, belongings, dated letters, references to real places etc. So, for instance, stories illustrated with photographs might be used. Again, it is preferable at this level to use stories set in the present or recent past rather than the distant past.

(c) show an awareness that different stories about the past can give different versions of what happened (LD 2).

Evidence of achievement: The child is able to retell a story or part of a story from another character's point of view (eg *A Balloon for Grandad*); or to detect differences in two children's accounts of a shared recent experience, eg a visit.

Comment: The important thing is the child's ability to empathise, to see things from another point of view, rather than chronological context.

(d) suggest reasons why people in the past acted as they did (LD 2).

Evidence of achievement: After listening to the stories, the child is able to indicate why, for example, Amrita Devi wanted to stop the forest from being cut down (*The People Who Hugged the Trees*); or why Jewish children had to go into hiding during the 1930s (*The Children We Remember*); or why Mary Seacole chose to go to where there was war (*Mary Seacole*).

Comment: Fictional stories which raise issues about characters' motives and behaviour could also be used.

(e) distinguish between a fact and a point of view. (LD 3).

Evidence of achievement: After listening to a historical story, the child is able to tell the difference between what really happened and opinions about characters and events. It might be helpful to draw up statements about the story, divided into 'fact' and 'point of view'.

2. Pictures

Teachers may wish to find out whether children can:

(a) communicate information acquired from an historical source (LD 1).

Evidence of achievement: The child talks about the photographs (see chapter six), picking out the historical details (eg the old-fashioned buses, horse-drawn vehicles and the clothes worn by people in the *Charing Cross Hotel* photograph.

(b) recognise that historical sources can stimulate and help answer questions about the past (LD 2).

Evidence of achievement: When talking about the photograph, the child asks questions, seeking to find out more about a particular aspect.

(c) identify differences between past and present times. (LDs 1-2)

Evidence of achievement: The child is able to indicate a number of differences between then and now from looking, for instance, at the photograph of *Children boarding a train*. A contemporary photograph on the same theme could be used to help the comparison.

(d) make deductions from historical sources (LD 3).

Evidence of achievement: The child makes a deduction from the evidence in a picture and suggests a reason for it (eg, referring to *The Mounted Prince* painting, 'I think this must be in India/Pakistan because sometimes my mum dresses like those ladies. I think it must be a long time ago because they had no cups...')

3. Artefacts

Teachers may wish to find out whether children can:

(a) communicate information acquired from a historical source (LD 1).

Evidence of achievement: While handling an artefact (section seven), the child describes some of its details.

(b) recognise that historical sources can stimulate and help answer questions about the past (LD 2).

Evidence of achievement: When investigating an artefact, the child asks a question about its use; or is able to relate the object to existing knowledge.

(c) identify differences between past and present times (LD 2).

Evidence of achievement: The child describes how an artefact differs from the equivalent used today; or draws and writes captions indicating some of the differences.

(d) make deductions from historical sources (LD 3).

Evidence of achievement: The child makes a deduction from the artefact and suggests a reason for it (eg 'I think this shoe must have been worn a lot because it's cracked and scratched.')

4. Historical change

Teachers may wish to find out whether children can:

(a) place familiar objects in chronological order (LDs 1, 2).

Evidence of achievement: the child correctly arranges a small number of artefacts into sets of 'new' 'old' and' very old'.

(b) describe changes over a period of time (LD 3).

Evidence of achievement: the child is able to describe, draw or write about a few of the differences between now and when his or her mum was a little girl.

(c) give a reason for a historical event or development (LD 3).

Evidence of achievement: the child is able to suggest a reason for why street lights have replaced lanterns; or for why some part of the area around their school has changed.

(d) identify differences between times in the past (LD 3).

Evidence of achievement: the child is able to describe one or two differences between 'a long time ago' (sometime this century) and 'a very long time ago' (previous centuries.) Some of the pictures in chapter five might be helpful.

Chapter eight

More stories and useful books

The stories suggested below can all be used in the ways suggested in chapter three. A synopsis is also included of the stories featured in the webs.

a. Fictional stories, myths and legends

1. Verna AARDEMA and Beatriz VIDAL
    Bringing the Rain to Kapiti Plain: An African Folktale
    Picturemacs 1986

All forms of life on Kapiti Plain are threatened by drought until the resourceful herdboy, Ki-pat, finds a way to bring the rain. Told in rhyme, this is a good story to discuss seasons (the differences between Britain and Africa) and the passing of time.

2. Indu ANAND and Hasna ISMAIL
    King Jahangir and the Baby: An Indian Tale
    Andre Deutsch 1988

A long time ago in India, two women come to the palace of Mughal King Jahangir with a baby that each claims is theirs. The story tells how the king finds out which is the real mother. Available in dual text —Urdu, Bengali, Panjabi, Gujerati, Arabic with English.

3. Ian BECK
Emily and the Golden Acorn
Doubleday/Transworld Publishers 1992

Emily's tree has magical qualities. When she makes a wish, the houses and gardens in front of her house are transformed into a shining sea. Emily and her brother Jack set sail on a pirate ship and embark on an exciting adventure. A good question for children is whether they think this story happens nowadays or a long time ago.

4. Peter BONNICI and Lisa KOPPER
The Festival
Mantra Publishing 1984

Arjuna usually finds visits to his grandmother's village boring but this time grandmother announces that it is time to start preparations for the special village festival. It is not a festival that Arjuna knows anything about but there will be something special in it for him. Available in dual text — Bengali, Gujerati, Urdu, Panjabi, all with English and on audiocassette.

5. Peter BONNICI and Lisa KOPPER
The First Rains
Mantra Publishing 1988

Amidst general doubts, Arjuna is sure that the rains will begin on time. The story evokes preparations for the monsoon season in India and its importance in the lives of ordinary people. A good story to discuss differences in seasonal patterns. Dual text available in Bengali, Gujerati, Panjabi with English, and on audiocassette.

6. Peter BONNICI and Lisa KOPPER
The Present
Mantra Publishing 1988

Grandpa in India writes to his granddaughters Geeta and Alice in England, relating how their cousins Amar and Meera went looking for a birthday present for their mother. A good story to link to 'the letter to grandparents' activity. Available in dual text — Urdu, Bengali, Gujerati, Panjabi with English.

7. Ruth BROWN
A Dark, Dark Tale
Red Fox Books 1992

A story set in the past: the magnificent illustrations take us first to a moor, then into a wood in which we see a house. We visit each room in the house until we run into something rather special. A simple read-aloud story which lends itself to be sequenced. Children will enjoy repeating 'dark, dark'.

8. Anthony BROWNE
Changes
Walker Books 1993

At 10.15 on Thursday morning Joseph's father tells him that things are going to change. And change they do: the bathroom turns into a person, the front wheel of his bicycle into an apple. Joseph hides in his room until, a little later, the door opens and in come his mother and father with a new baby sister. The exquisite pictures make this a very appropriate story to explore children's perceptions of change.

This story can be supported by the excellent information book *Changes* by Joanne JESSOP (Wayland Publishers 1992) which illustrates changes in nature, people and the wider world.

9. Crescent DRAGONWAGON and Jerry PINKNEY
    Half a Moon and One Whole Star
    Bodley Head 1987

A celebration of the rich mysterious world of night. In bed but not yet asleep on a summer's evening, Susan breathes in green smells, hears the night-time world unfolding around her and anticipates some of the things that will happen in the morning.. Lovely poetic text.

10. Crescent DRAGONWAGON and Jerry PINKNEY
    Home Place
    Macmillan Publishing Co. USA 1990

A beautifully original story about the passage of time, family generations, change and continuity. A family out hiking discover little clues about another family who lived there a long time ago. Or did they? Are they real or imagined? Vividly illustrated, this is an excellent story to raise the issue of historical sources, ie ' how do we know about people who lived a long time before us?'

11. Valerie FLOURNOY and Jerry PINKNEY
    The Patchwork Quilt
    Picture Puffins Penguin Books 1987

A year in the life of a black American family is reflected in the colourful patchwork quilt that Grandma makes, watched by little Tanya. When Grandma falls ill, Tanya takes over and comes to understand the significance of the quilt to her family's history.

12. Michael FOREMAN
    Ben's Baby
    Magi Publications 1989

Little Ben wants a baby for his next birthday. The story takes us through events in Ben's life as the seasons change and the year passes, until he gets his wish. Available in dual text — Vietnamese, Chinese, Greek. Urdu, Bengali, Gujerati, Panjabi, Hindi, all with English.

13. Michael FOREMAN
    Grandfather's Pencil
    Anderson Press 1993

Around the turn of the century a little boy lies asleep somewhere in the city. While he sleeps his pencil begins to write, journeying back to the time when it was a tall tree in a forest, its branches rustled by the wind. Then in turn, the paper, the table and the floorboards tell their tales...

14. Deborah GOULD
    Grandpa's Slide Show
    Picture Puffin 1990

Sam and Douglas always look forward to Grandpa's slide show. When he dies, they are helped to understand and accept their loss by looking at family photographs. The story emphasises the importance of photographs in preserving memories and histories.

15. Nigel GRAY
A Balloon for Grandad
Collins Picture Lions 1988

As Sam's colourful balloon escapes from his home, his dad helps him imagine its adventurous journey to a far-away island where his grandad Abdulla lives. The lovely illustrations and rich language convey the feelings of a child for a grandparent who lives far away.

16. Eloise GREENFIELD and Floyd COOPER
Grandpa's Face
Hutchinson Children's Books 1989

Tamika loved Grandpa's face. It told everything about him. One evening, while he is rehearsing for a play, Tamika sees him pull a face that she has never seen before and becomes frightened. A thoughtful statement about how children perceive changes in people and how fragile is their sense of security.

17. Mairi HEDDERWICK
Katie Morag and the Two Grandmothers
Picture Lions 1988

Katie Morag lives in a Scottish island home and has two grandmas: Grandma Island and Grandma Mainland, who comes to stay for a holiday. Gradually the two grandmas come to appreciate one another's very different lifestyles.

18. Pat HUTCHINS
Clocks and More Clocks
Bodley Head Children's Books 1970

Mr Higgins's anxiety to know the right time leads him to install a variety of clocks on each floor of his large house but they never seem to tell the same time. A hilarious story, excellent for discussing children's basic experiences of time.

19. Aleph KEMAL and Frane LESSAC
The Bird who was an Elephant
Cambridge University Press 1989

A day in the life of an Indian village through the eyes of a bird. The bird swoops in from the desert and visits the palmist in order to find out his past and his future. Colourful paintings illustrate the story. Available in dual text — Urdu, Bengali, Gujarati, Panjabi with English.

20. Virginia KROLL and Nancy CARPENTER
Masai and I
Hamish Hamilton 1993

A story that celebrates empathy and imagination. At school one day Linda, an English girl, learns about East Africa and a people called the Masai. Linda reflects and imagines what her life would be like if she were a Masai girl. A brilliant story that makes a very positive statement about cultural difference.

21. Ann LINDEN and Lynne RUSSELL
One Smiling Grandma
William Heinemann 1992

A little girl spends her holiday with her grandma in the Caribbean. As they make their way to the market, listen to the exciting sounds of the steel drums, collect conch shells on the beach and watch the fish glide through the air, they play a special counting game that will bring back the memories of their time together. Superbly illustrated.

22. Amanda LOVERSEED
Tickatoo's Journey: An Eskimo folktale
Blackie Books 1990

An ice spirit enters the heart of Nanook, the village's oldest and wisest man, and soon he becomes gravely ill. Only a flame from the sun can save him. Brave Tickatoo, his grandson, offers to make the dangerous journey.

23. Moy MCCRORY and Eleni MICHAEL
Grandmother's Tale
Magi Publications 1989

Every Friday when Nazan and her grandmother go to market, her grandmother tells her a story. On this occasion it is about long ago in Turkey when Grandmother's baby sister was born. A good story to tell before the visit of a grandparent to the classroom and for discussing facts and points of view. Available in dual text — Panjabi, Bengali, Urdu, Gujerati, Hindi, Greek, all with English.

24. Florence Heide PARRY and Judith Gilliland HEIDE
The Day of Ahmed's Secret
Victor Gollanz 1992

Ahmed travels through the streets of Cairo delivering gas cannisters to elderly people. Returning home at the end of a working day, he reveals his secret: he has learned to write his name. A very good story to discuss names/naming ceremonies and their meaning, and for writing in different scripts.

25. Saviour PIROTTA and Mrinal MITRA
Do You Believe in Magic?
Mantra Publishing 1990

Sumed brings a seashell into the classroom from his holiday in India. All his friends take turns to listen to its sounds except Miss Wicks, the teacher, who will not use her imagination. Available in dual text — Urdu, Gujarati, Bengali, Chinese, Arabic with English.

26. Marieluise RITTER
Mum's Strike
Magi Publications 1989

A good story about home routines, featuring a single mother and her children. Mum decides to go on strike when she discovers the mess that the children have made. The story is about how the children learn from this experience. Available in dual text — Bengali, Urdu, Gujerati, Panjabi with English.

27. Paul and Emma ROGERS and Priscilla Lamont
Our House
Walker Books 1991

The history of a house is told through little episodes in the lives of its occupants from the distant past to the present: 1780 Welcome; 1840 Father's late; 1910 Wait and See; 1990 Where's Henry? The illustrations convey the changes in the house and its immediate environment.

28. Deborah Lee ROSE and Birgitta SAFLUND
The People Who Hugged the Trees
Roberts Reinhart International 1990

The story of the first Chipko (meaning 'hug-the-tree') people. Centuries ago in India a young girl, Amrita Devi, inspired her village community to stand up to the king and his axemen, and prevent their forest from being cut down. Beautifully illustrated with water-colours of rural Rajasthan.

29. Kamiko SAKAI and Tomie ARAI
Sachiko Means Happiness
Children's Book Press USA 1990

When Sachiko was born her happy grandmother gave her her own name, which means 'happiness' in Japanese. But now Grandmother has changed greatly. A story that sensitively depicts the frailties of age.

30. Kiki and Kathryn SHAW
Maya and the Town that Loved a Tree
Children's Universe, Rizoli International Publications 1992

Once upon a time there was a little town whose people were very happy and where the sky was clear and blue. But as it grew into a big city, the sky turned grey and there was no air nor love for anything alive and green. A little girl, Maya, teaches the people to change their ways. A good story to tell before *The People who Hugged the Trees* and for discussing the issue of history as progress — 'do things always change for the better?'

31. Dyan SHELDON and Gary BLYTHE
The Garden
Hutchinson Children's Books 1993

When Jenny discovers a flint in her garden probably hundreds of years old, she tries to imagine the land when there were no houses or towns or busy roads but fields peopled by Native Americans, singing and telling stories in the firelight.

32. Rani and Jugnu SINGH and Biman MULLICK
The Amazing Adventures of Hanuman
Based on the ancient Indian epic poem *The Ramayana*
BBC Books 1988

The most accesible version of the story of Rama and Sita, told with a good deal of humour. Here, Hanuman, half-monkey and half- human, helps Rama search for the princess Sita, kidnapped by the demon king Ravana. Children will find the colourful illustrations particularly appealing.

33. John STEPTOE
Mufaro's Beautiful Daughters: An African Folktale
Hamish Hamilton 1988

A story of two girls, Manyara and Nyasha, in Africa of long ago. Their father Mufaro wants them to appear before the king, who is seeking a bride. The story tells of their very different reactions and very different rewards. Beautifully illustrated.

34. Colin THOMPSON
The Paperbag Prince
Julia MacRae Publishing 1992

The Paperbag Prince is an old man who lives in a disused railway carriage at the end of a town dump. As he reflects on the folly of the townspeople who dump their rubbish in the middle of a beautiful green valley, time passes and the seasons change until one day the refuse trucks stop coming. The wonderfully detailed illustrations make this book an absolute treat.

35. Ann TOMPERT and Robert Andrew PARKER
Grandfather Tang's Story
Julia MacRae Books 1990

A traditional Chinese story told using tangrams (Chinese puzzle squares) by a grandfather to his grandchildren.

36. Martin WADDELL and Angela BARRETT
The Hidden House
Walker Books 1990

Three wooden dolls are left all alone when the owner of the hidden house leaves, never to return. But things get better when other occupants arrive and give the place a new lease of life.

37. Martin WADDELL and Jane JOHNSON
Grandma's Bill
Simon and Schuster 1990

Every Thursday Bill goes to tea with his Grandma. One day she takes down her big book of photographs and together they look at the pictures of the past. A story told with warmth and humour, dealing reassuringly with loss.

38. Martin WADDELL and Terry MILNE
The Toymaker
Walker Books 1991

An original treatment in two parts. 'Once upon a time' we find little Mary playing in the toy shop with the dolls specially made for her by her father, Matthew. 'Once upon another time' we see Mary as a grandma, returning to the toy shop with her granddaughter and reflecting on the changes brought about by the passage of time.

39. Jill Paton WALSH and Sophy WILLIAMS
When Grandma Came
Viking Penguin 1992

Madeleine's grandma has travelled the world and seen wonders in the Arctic, Africa, Australia, India, Egypt. But always she returns to assure her little granddaughter that she is the greatest wonder of all. A magnificently illustrated story about the bond between young and old.

40. Rosalma ZUBIZARETTA, Harriet ROHMER, David SCHECTER and Fernando OLIVERA
The Woman Who Outshone the Sun: A Mexican Folktale
Children's Book Press USA 1991

In Mexico long ago, a woman with thick, shining black hair and an iguana at her side, arrives in a mountain village. She is respected by the village elders for knowing the ways of nature but others are not very nice to her. The story tells of the legend of Lucia Zentano and how she won the villagers over... Available in dual text — Spanish with English.

b. Stories about real happenings and historical events

There is a dearth of good, accessible stories of this kind for children. Here are some that can be used, for example, to contrast fictional characters and real people.

1. Chana Byers ABELLS
The Children We Remember
Julia MacRae Books Franklyn Watts 1987

A moving and accesible tale of courage and endurance. It tells through photographs about the Jewish children who lived and died during the Holocaust.

2. Sylvia COLLICOTT
Mary Seacole
Ginn History Stories, Ginn and Co. 1991

The story of Mary Seacole who went on her own initiative to nurse the sick and wounded soldiers during the Crimean War (1854-56) after being refused permission by the British Government to go as one of Florence Nightingale's nurses.

3. Feroza MATHIESON
The Very Hot Samosas
A&C Black 1989

A story set in Pakistan as a family prepare for a meal. Photographic illustrations.

4. Feroza MATHIESON
The Missing Money
A & C Black 1989

A photographically illustrated story set in Pakistan on the 'Lost and Found' theme.

5. Feroza MATHIESON
Parni's Birthday Surprise
A & C Black 1988

Set in India, the story describes a little girl's birthday treat.

6. Anne ROWE
A War Christmas
Ginn History Stories, Ginn and Co. 1991

A story of two children evacuated from London during the Second World War and sent to live with a couple in the countryside. Illustrations convey a sense of the period.

7. Ailsa and Alan SCARSBROOK
First Day at School
A & C Black 1987

The story of Saiqa and Michael's first day at school. Photographic illustrations.

8. Susheila STONE
Nadeem Makes Samosas
Evans Brothers 1987

An English/Urdu dual language story about mealtime routines.

9. Ming TSOW
A Day with Ling
Hamish Hamilton 1982

Anne spends the day with her friend Ling. Photographic illustrations.

10. Renu Nagrath WOODBRIDGE
Stir-Fry
A & C Black 1989

When Rachel's class decides to cook a giant stir-fry, everyone brings a different vegetable from home. Photographic illustrations.

c. Information books for children about the past

A & C Black (PO Box 19, Huntingdon, Cambs, P.19 3SF) have produced an attractive series for younger children, *History Mysteries*. Each book has a different theme and the past is brought alive through colour photographs of mystery objects from the 1900s, 1930s and 1960s. Children are encouraged to look for clues in each photograph and to guess what the object is. The object is revealed on the following page.

The following are available to date:

Washing
At School
Travelling
Cooking
Getting Dressed
Shopping
Toys

An excellent resource to support children's work with pictures and artefacts (chapters six and seven).

Chapter nine

Finding out more...

Stories

Other lists of storybooks that are particularly relevant for the historical dimension of the curriculum can be found in the following publications:

Kath COX and Pat HUGHES
Early Years History: An Approach Through Story
Liverpool Institute of Higher Education 1990
An updated list is also available from Pat Hughes at the Liverpool Institute of Higher Education.

Eric MADDERN
A Teacher's Guide to Storytelling at Historic Sites
English Heritage 1992

Chris ROUTH and Anne ROWE
Stories for Time: Resourcing the History Curriculum for Key Stage 1
Reading and Language Information Centre, University of Reading 1992

Ann ROWE and Chris ROUTH
A Place for Stories
Reading and Language Information Centre,
University of Reading 1992

Also more generally useful are:
Stories as Starting Points for Design and Technology
Design Council Education 1989 (Design Council Educational, PO Box 10, Weatherby LS23 7EL.)

Tony AYLWIN
Traditional Storytelling and Education: a Directory of Storytellers
School of Primary Education, University of Greenwich 1992

Hilary HESTER
Stories in the Multilingual Primary Classroom
ILEA 1983 (Harcourt, Brace, Jovanovich or from the Centre for Language in Primary Education, Webber Row, London SE1 8QW.)

Bilingual resources

C. Hoffman's *An Introduction to Bilingualism* (Longman 1991) is a useful starting point for understanding the positive educational consequences of knowing more than one language.

Adrian Blackledge has edited a bok by educators working with bilingual children in anglophone countries: *Teaching Bilingual Children* (Trentham Books 1994).

Most of the bilingual stories listed in this pack are published by Mantra Publishing, 5 Alexandra Grove, London, N12 8NU or Magi Publications, 55 Crowland Avenue, Hayes, Middx UB3 4JP.

Soma Books (38 Kennington Lane, London SE11 4LS) are leading stockists of bilingual resources and produce a comprehensive list of dual language books currently in print. They also stock a useful collection of dolls, shadow puppets, printing blocks, crafts and fabrics.

Letterbox Library (Unit 2D, Leroy House, 436 Essex Road, London N 1 3QP) provides an excellent selection of the most recent multicultural, non-sexist children's books, which it offers at good discounts. Titles include a range of bilingual stories. The books are listed in an informative quarterly catalogue, available to subscribers from the address above.

The Primary Learning Record was developed at the Centre for Language in Primary Education and described in *Guide to the Primary Learning Record* by Hilary Hester with Sue Ellis and Myra Barrs, 1993, CLPE, Webber Row, London SE 1 8QW.

There are now increasing facilities for multilingual wordprocessing. The Allwrite programme's current range of languages includes Arabic, Bengali, Cantonese, Croatian, French, Farsi, Gaelic, German, Greek, Gujarati, Hindi, Italian,

Panjabi, Portuguese, Russian, Serbian, Spanish, Tamil, Turkish, Urdu, Vietnamese and Welsh. It runs on the RM Nimbus range of computers. The package is available from LETTS, John Ruskin Street, London SE5 OPQ. There is a telephone support services for users (071- 587-0985).

Susanna Steele and Penny Robertson of Grasmere Primary School, East London have written a thoughtful account of bilingual wordprocessing in the classroom: 'Tapping into Allwrite: Turkish is part of what I am' in *Language Matters* 1991/92 No 3 (issue on *Bilingualism in practice*) available from the Centre for Language in Primary Education.

Liverpool Education Directorate's Race Equality team have produced a dual language booklet — English and Somali — *Exploring History*. Illustrated with photographs of children from a variety of backgrounds, it is designed to help teachers value a range of different histories at Key Stage 1.

Also worth looking at is Susheila Stone 'Supporting Bilingualism' in *Child Education* August 1990.

Parents

Sheila Wolfendale's *Empowering Parents and Teachers: Working for Children* (Cassell 1992) provides the most detailed up-to-date analysis of parental involvement in home-school links and explores parents' contributions to school processes. Also useful are:

Wendy BLOOM
Partership with Parents in Reading
Hodder and Stoughton 1987

J. ATKIN, J. BASTIANI and J. GOODE
Listening to Parents: An approach to the improvement of home-school relations
Croom Helm 1988

Susheila STONE
'Involving Ethnic Minority Parents' in
Child Education May 1991

Sylvia COLLICOTT
'What's in a name?' in
Child Education September 1987 discusses naming systems and meanings.

Viv EDWARDS and Angela REDFERN
At Home in School: Parent participation in Primary Education
Routledge 1988

Artefacts and Family History

The Hackney Schools' Study Collection (HSSC) have assembled a diverse collection of artefacts for children to handle and explore, available to all schools in north London. Items include early gramophones, cookers, old newspapers, magazines, posters and photographs. HSSC is based at Hackney Professional Development Centre, Queensbridge Building, Albion Drive, Hackney, London E8 4ET.

Gail DURBIN, Susan MORRIS and Sue WILKINSON
A Teacher's Guide to Learning from Objects
English Heritage 1990

Evaluating Artefacts
Centre for Multicultural Education, Harrison Road,
Leicester LE4 6RB

Back to Your Roots. Recording your family history
BBC Education 1993 Useful booklet accompanying the oral history series on childhood 1900-1950, *A Labour of Love* broadcast in early 1993.

The pictures in this book

On the social history of the Suffragette Movement see Diana Atkinson's *The Purple, White and Green: Suffragettes in London 1906-1914* (Museum of London 1992).

Sheila Taylor's *A Journey Through Time; London Transport Photographs 1880 to 1965* (London Transport Museum 1992) is an excellent pictorial history of changes in modes of transport over the last hundred years.

Beautifully illustrated accounts of the development of Indian visual art can be found in J.M. Rogers *Mughal Miniatures* (British Museum Press 1993) and John Guy and Deborah Swallow *Arts of India 1550-1990* (V & A 1990).

Museums

Visits often provide an inspiring change of scenery, prompting children to volunteer their knowledge and experiences far more than they do in the classroom.

As a source of learning from images, artefacts and exhibitions, museums can offer a worthwhile historical experience for children. It is best to check with your local museum service regarding loans and teaching sessions geared to children at Key Stage 1. It is usually necessary to book a term in advance.

The best national guide to museums is the *Exploring Museums* series published by HMSO PO Box 276, London SW8 5DT and available from HMSO regional bookshops. It lists the most interesting museums in the British Isles region by region.

Here is a small sample of interesting museums which loan artefacts (L) and/or run teaching sessions (T):

Commonwealth Institute
Kensington High Street, London W8 6NQ (T)
Has a well-stocked Resource Library which teachers can visit. Also organises some teaching sessions for children as well as workshops and conferences for teachers on specific aspects of life in Commonwealth countries. Holds events for school groups during major festivals (Diwali, Christmas, Carnival, etc).

Also at
Commononwealth Institute Northern Regional Centre,
Salt Mill, Saltaire, Shipley, Bradford, West Yorkshire BD18 3LB.

The Museum of London,
London Wall, London EC2Y 5HN (T)
Collections devoted to telling the story of London and its people. The Education Department runs teaching sessions (see chapter seven) and the museum also holds some interesting exhibitions on aspects of the social history of the capital.

The Grange Museum of Community History
Neasden Lane, London NW 10 1 BQ
(LT for schools in the borough of Brent only.)
Focuses on local history, reflecting the multicultural composition of the borough. The teaching sessions centre on domestic artefacts, toys and games and aspects of local history.

The Horniman Museum and Library
100 London Road, Forest Hill, London SE23 3PQ (LT)
A varied collection on customs and beliefs, arts and crafts. Runs family events (eg shoe-making with paper and clay) during holidays.

Victoria & Albert Museum

South Kensington, London SW7 2RL (T)

Specialising in the decorative arts, with major galleries devoted to European, Indian, Japanese, Chinese, Korean and Islamic art. Teaching sessions vary in theme. Family events during school holidays. Fre publications include a time-line for children.

London Transport Museum

Covent Garden, London WC2E 7BB (T)

The history of London's transport, treated not simply in mechanical terms but as a social phenomenon. The museum looks at the effects of public transport on human life.

Geffrye Museum

Kingsland Road, London E2 8EA (T)

Located in 18th century almshouses in lovely gardens. Visitors can walk through a series of English domestic period rooms from 1600 to the 1950s.

The North of England Open Air Museum

Beamish, County Durham DH9 0RG (LT).

An experience of history from below that brings to life the sense of community of the mining pit villages which once dominated the north-east. Activities for children.

Welsh Folk Museum

St. Fagans, Cardiff CF5 6XB (T)

An authentic picture of the cultural life of the Welsh people through the centuries. An exciting open air museum where children can descend down an old mine.

New Lanark Conservation

New Lanark Mills, Lanark, Scotland ML11 9DB (T)

A memorable visit. Includes the 'Annie McLeod Experience' — a ten year-old mill girl in Robert Owen's 19th Century New Lanark settlement telling her story. Children can dress up, handle old household and manufacturing objects (e.g. raw cotton, bobbins) and toys.

The Ironbridge Gorge Museum,

Ironbridge, Telford, Shropshire. (LT)

Hands-on experience of what life was like during the momentous years of the industrial revolution. Indoor and out, complete with old-style geese.

Acton Scott Historic Working Farm

Wenlock Lodge, Acton Scott, Near Church Stretton, Shropshire SY6 6QN. (T) Experience an upland farm at the turn of the century. Daily demonstrations of rural craft provide an insight into estate life a hundred years ago.

Museum of Transport

Kelvin Hall,1 Bunhouse Road, Glasgow G3 8DP. (T)

An inviting modern museum which conveys the excitement of travel. Atmospheric displays focus on the different forms of transport from the Victorian era to present day Scotland.

National Museum of Photography, Film and Television

Princes View, Bradford, West Yorkshire BD5 0TR. (T)

Relates the history of the moving image. Children can handle old cameras, lights and a range of early media equipment.

Birmingham Museum and Art Gallery

Chamberlain Square, Birmingham B3 3DH. (LT)

Loans a wide range of artefacts to schools. Children can look at and handle fabrics and designs from a variety of cultures.

Merseyside Maritime Museum
Albert Dock, Liverpool L3 4AA. (T)
Spread over six dockside locations, the museum's 1840 architecture houses the country's largest permanent exhibition on the influence of the slave trade and its legacy in enriching European and American cultures.

Merseyside Museum of Labour History
Islington, Liverpool L3 3EE. (T)
Records the changing nature of work and tells the story of working men and women over the last centuries.

Oldham Art Gallery and Local Interest Museum
Greaves Street, Oldham OL1 1 DN . (LT)
Organises events and exhibitions on various aspects of local life in the past.

Local History

Local history societies, museum and library services often produce pictorial records of the local area. Recent work on the London area includes:

Nick MERRIMAN (Ed.)
The Peopling of London; Fifteen Thousand Years of Settlement From Overseas.
Museum of London 1993
Shows how London has had a cosmopolitan population from its very beginnings

Valerie HART, Richard KNIGHT and Lesley MARSHALL
Camden Town 1791-1991: A Pictorial Record
London Borough of Camden, Leisure Services Department 1991

Ian BRADLEY, June BROUGHTON and Douglas CLUETT
All Our Yesterdays
Sutton Leisure Services 1991. A pictorial record of the London Borough of Sutton over the last century.

David MANDER
The London Borough of Hackney in Old Photographs
Allan Sutton 1989

J. FISHMAN and N. BREACH
The Streets of East London
Duckworth 1979

Paul BARKSHIRE
London Villages
Lennard Publishing 1992
Contemporary photographs of hidden villages and country houses in present day London.

Miscellaneous

As a popular activity in the classroom, cooking can also include a historical dimension. The following books may be of interest:

Jo LAWRIE
Pot Luck: Cooking and recipes from the past
A & C Black 1991

Maggie BLACK
The Medieval Cookbook
British Museum Press 199

Marieke CLARKE
Recipes from Around the World
Oxfam Education Deparment 1983

Jennifer DAVIES
The Wartime Kitchen and Garden
BBC Books 1993

Michelle BERRIDALE-JOHNSON
The British Museum Cookbook
British Museum Press 1987